professional *perspectives*

Series Editor **Mike Burghall**

Creating Conversation in Class

Chris Sion

DELTA
PUBLISHING

Published by
DELTA PUBLISHING
39 Alexandra Road
Addlestone
Surrey KT15 2PQ

First published 2001
Reprinted 2005

ISBN 0 953309 88 6

Designed by Christine Cox
Cover illustration by Phillip Burrows
Project managed by Chris Hartley
Printed by Halstan & Co, Amersham

Acknowledgements
The publishers would like to thank Tanya Whatling for her
valuable editorial contribution.

This book is dedicated to the memory of Saxon Menné.

Foreword

Creating Conversation in Class is a collection of interesting and unusual ideas for students of English to discuss. The majority of the activities are intermediate, although many can easily be adapted to both higher and lower levels. They require only a minimum of preparation and very few materials. The materials may be used for classes in which the whole period is devoted to discussion, as well as for shorter sessions within a larger lesson.

The book attempts to address the needs of adult students who are unsure of themselves in an English conversation once they have exchanged greetings, reported on the quality of their flight and commented on the weather. At the same time, it provides younger learners with the stimulus to talk about their own interests and helps them develop the confidence to talk about themselves.

Conversation may be loosely defined as 'an informal, spoken exchange of information, opinions, anecdotes and ideas'. *Creating Conversation in Class* is designed to help students cope with the question, 'What do I say now?'

There is a tradition in which a topic or role-play is presented to the class, often out of the blue, along with a list of vocabulary and structures to be practised. Many teachers and coursebooks proceed in this way: it is neat and controlled and the objectives are clear. However, in my experience, it frequently generates resistance to the very teaching points you set out to practise. Students hurry through the activities as quickly as they can. They proudly announce, 'We've finished', heave a sigh of relief, and then go on to talk about something else, in which they are genuinely interested, with far more commitment.

The alternative to this is a combination of introducing topics indirectly, building them up slowly, relating them to the students' lives, entering into a dialogue with the class and being prepared to experiment. *Creating Conversation in Class* suggests there is a need to be flexible and, above all, develop the art of using seemingly inconsequential moments and ideas to create conversation and get your students talking. I hope it succeeds.

Chris Sion

Contents

The Art of Creating Conversation

When I started teaching, I used to spend hours on careful preparation. I can still remember pasting dozens of pictures onto cardboard to make flashcards, hunting for examples and scrupulously scripting every moment of each lesson. If I got one correct sentence back in a conversation with a student, I felt fulfilled.

Some years later, teaching a low intermediate group of faltering German businessmen, I simply told them to work in pairs and talk about what they had to do at work the following week. They talked English non-stop for 45 minutes, only occasionally turning to me for help.

Our task as teachers is to find the key that creates and unlocks the students' need to communicate. Students who don't like to be put on the spot will latch on to throwaway comments, apparently irrelevant tasks, puzzles, games, questions and conversation topics if they are carefully introduced and unobtrusively built up. Conversation needs to be drawn out of students rather than pumped into them. We need to balance preparation and spontaneity.

Small talk and big talk

As a university student, I used to be quite cynical about making small talk and what I regarded as meaningless conversational exchanges. I preferred to talk about substantial issues and get immediately involved in academic debate. Over the years, however, I have come to realise that people do not generally respond favourably to 'Good morning and what do you think is the meaning of life?' Small talk is a necessary ingredient in deepening social interaction. It is a first step towards 'big' talk.

My assumption is that students do have something to say; that, just like 'real people', they enjoy talking about themselves, their families, their interests, backgrounds, jobs, plans, dreams and frustrations; about what they had for lunch, where they do their shopping ... as well as if there is a God.

In a social situation such as a party, if the conversation flags, I sometimes throw out a comment like, 'What's the difference between a fruit and a vegetable?' or 'What was the naughtiest thing you ever did as a child?' Lively exchanges and interesting reactions invariably ensue. In much the same way, I might casually remark in class: 'Do teddy bears have souls?' and see how the conversation develops.

A favourite classroom strategy of mine is to elicit a handful of unconnected topics from the students: discotheques; mobile phones; the general election; neighbours; the bus strike; tennis rackets and cloning human beings, for example. I then let pairs choose what they want to talk about. Totally unstructured. Just like real life. I recently found one student asking another advice about buying Russian icons. This is the way it should be: genuine interaction about a common interest. It is simply not the case that a conversation has to be structured in order to be valuable, with the topic introduced, developed and recapitulated. Here we are concerned with the free stage. No matter how trivial or obscure a topic, if it gets the students talking English we will have succeeded in creating conversation.

Accuracy and fluency

This relatively unstructured approach of *Creating Conversation in Class* raises the issue of when and where to correct students. Obviously, you should pay close attention to students' errors and consider carefully the most effective moment and manner to correct them. Equally obviously, when students make mistakes, you should not constantly interrupt them to put them down in mid-sentence. It is far more effective to echo the correct version back to them.

More important than rigorous correction of their errors is paying attention to the students themselves and creating a feeling of self-esteem amongst them. When they are working in pairs, you should move around the class listening and responding to what they have to say, not just checking the quality of their language. They should not be given the impression they are being obliged to do pairwork simply to fill the time.

Creating Conversation in Class focuses on fluency, not accuracy, which is dealt with in a myriad of other sources. Fluency, accuracy and substance all have a place in language learning. Correction is important, particularly to those students who believe they learn from being corrected. But it is debatable whether the value lies in the correction itself or in the students' perception that their errors have been recognised. There is even a danger that by paying repeated attention to errors you could unintentionally be reinforcing them. The crucial factor is establishing yourself as a teacher who is in tune with your students and aware of their needs.

Learning to learn

Creating Conversation in Class also focuses on learning to learn in Learner Training sections A - E. It is important for students to be aware of their learning preferences and the teacher can make this awareness into the subject of extremely interesting and creative conversations. Study skills don't have to be dry and prescriptive. They, too, can be developed creatively by the teacher and become part of the art of creating conversation.

Using This Book

Each activity mentions the linguistic functions it practises, indicates the recommended time and level, and details the materials required. Any necessary preparation is outlined.

The instructions are presented as lesson skeletons, which you are invited to flesh out, taking your own teaching situation into account. Not all possibilities can be included. However, there are some general strategies that you can use to make these skeletons come to life.

1 Tailoring the activities to suit your classes

- **Use your common sense.** This is the most important ingredient. If you do *Morris and Boris* (page 92), which deals with comparisons, you should have already covered the comparative form and you might want to revise it before beginning the activity. Self-evident points such as these are not usually mentioned.

- **Relate the activities to your students' interests.** Don't do *General Motors* (page 48), which requires students to talk about their cars, with children or with a class of adults who don't have cars. Try to connect activities with what is happening in the students' everyday lives. For instance, an incident where one student blames another can serve as the occasion for doing *It's All Your Fault* (page 80).

- **Be flexible.** This is essential to creating lively conversation in class. If you want your students to talk about their jobs and some are unemployed or are studying full-time, let them talk about a job they used to do or about somebody else's job, or about a job they would like to have. Someone who is unemployed might nevertheless be involved in voluntary work and a college student could perhaps relate some material to the organisation of the college. (See *Personal and Professional*, page 24, for example).

- **Be tactful.** Remember that students may have very different jobs and come from quite different social backgrounds. You need to be particularly diplomatic with the activities connected with families. Personal circumstances and cultural factors will greatly affect students' attitudes to what they are asked to discuss. (See *Family Values*, page 79, for example.)

2 Starting and ending the lesson

A great deal of authentic conversation takes place inside the classroom but outside the formal parameters of the lesson. This is the 'twilight' time just before and after the lesson itself. This can be invaluable learning time. It is often more interesting than the main part of the lesson, in much the same way that Question Time, at the end of a lecture, can be more gripping than the lecture itself.

To develop this idea of interaction, *Getting Started* (page 16) suggests a useful collection of sixty ways of starting a lesson. Similarly, it is important that you use the time at the end of your lessons productively. Give your full attention to students who come up to you when the class is over.

3 Setting the scene

- **Introduce the topics slowly.** If you want to talk about Shakespeare, start with a simple quiz about him or give the students two minutes to list as many of his plays as they can. It's worth hunting out your old postcard of Stratford-upon-Avon and obtaining some other visuals. But don't start every lesson with a quiz and a postcard!

- **Vary your approach.** Keep the students wondering what's going to happen next. Wherever possible, link the activities to what you've been doing in class and to what is going on in 'the outside world'.

- **Use your voice, silence, pacing, timing and gesture** in developing an activity. Carefully chosen background music can play a valuable part in setting the mood. There's nothing like a little Scott Joplin to get the students moving around, or some quiet classical guitar music to settle them down for a reflective paired activity.

4 Organising pairwork

Practically every activity asks you to divide the class into pairs. Pairwork is the lifeblood of a student-centred conversation class. To maintain students' interest, it is important to vary the partners your students are being asked to work with, ideally giving them the chance of working with all the other students in the class during a course.

Twenty ways to organise pairs

- neighbours
- neighbours on the other side
- graded: stronger students helping weaker ones
- graded: stronger with stronger, weaker with weaker

- male with female

- female with female, male with male

- students who have never worked together before

- students who haven't worked together for a long time

- students who relate well with each other

- students from different countries

- students who speak different languages

- drawing students' names from a hat

- teacher decides: Cordelia and Jamie, Eric and Marianne

- friends

- students who don't know each other well

- students with common interests

- students with a common feature (long hair, blue eyes, jeans, beards, glasses, birthdays in July, supporters of the same football team)

- counting around the class, for example in a class of ten, number the students 1-2-3-4-5 and 1-2-3-4-5; pair the 1's, the 2's and so on

- as above, but using the alphabet instead of numbers

- hand the choice over to the students: let them decide

- **Odd numbers in a class.** If there is an odd number of students when you want to do pairwork, work with the extra student yourself. The only disadvantage is that you can't keep such a close eye on the others. Another option is to have one group of three to accommodate the extra student. Or you might decide to do the activity in groups of three instead of pairs. Most activities which call for

pairwork may be done with larger groups. The instructions do not always say, 'This step may be done in pairs, small groups or with the whole class'. The decision is yours.

5 Reporting back

- **Organisation.** Your students can report back to a second partner what they originally discussed with somebody else. You may prefer to get them to report back systematically or not. An advantage of doing it systematically is that everyone knows when their turn is and there is less chance of domination by the class extroverts. A disadvantage is that it is a less spontaneous. I sometimes say, 'Let's start with someone who doesn't usually start', or follow the students' ages or birthdays. Remember that some students like to be asked or invited to contribute. Observe them closely and react to what you see: 'Bill, you look thoughtful ... ', 'Joyce, you sounded angry … '

- **The need for discretion.** If pairs discuss a personal topic and are then required to report back to the class, it is important that confidences are not betrayed. I might be prepared to share a personal matter with a partner which I would not want disclosed to the whole group.

- **When one pair finishes.** The final practical point in dealing with pairwork and groupwork is what to do when one pair or group finishes before another. The answer is simple: just tell them to keep on making conversation in English.

6 The instructions

- **Preparation.** Most activities call for little or no preparation. Where they do, this is indicated under the 'Before Class' heading. Bear in mind that hours of planning may yield no more than a couple of minutes' discussion in class, whereas a casual comment may generate a whole lesson. Paradoxically, although some topics need to be built up slowly and carefully, simply saying, 'I've just bought a new computer. Has anyone else got Windows 2000? Did you have any problems installing it?' may well yield excellent results.

- **Personalisation.** Be prepared, too, to begin by talking about yourself to your group. This does not mean you have to divulge your most intimate secrets. Just give a demonstration so that the class knows what is required. For instance, in tackling *The Holidays* (page 32), spend a couple of minutes briefly talking about your own vacation. Or with *May I Introduce Myself?* (page 23), if you set a good example yourself, mixing general and personal information and showing that you have a sense of humour, the rewards will come in the students' reactions.

- **Time.** The time specifications are guidelines and are not intended to be followed exactly. In an activity like *The People in Your Life* (page 54) one student may talk about one person for ten minutes while their partner talks about ten different people for one minute each. It doesn't matter, as long as they are talking English. It is crucial that the students appreciate that the activities are springboards, departure points to be discussed, developed and even digressed from. One word answers are not sufficient.

- **Pace.** You need to take your circumstances into careful account. Doing an activity on a summer course in England, with a dozen students receiving five hours tuition every day, is clearly not the same as attempting it with forty pupils in a secondary school classroom in their single period of English per week. You have to adapt.

- **Level.** The majority of the activities are intermediate. However, the level specified is only a general indication. Take an activity like *Family Values* (page 79). An intermediate group might talk about this subject for twenty to thirty minutes with a rather restricted vocabulary. An advanced group would manage forty-five minutes or even an hour, using a much richer range of expression.

- **Expectations.** While you might not think your students' level is up to discussing some of the topics, you may be surprised to find that if you build up an activity slowly, so as to capture their interest, they *will* want to talk about it. They may be stretched, the vocabulary and grammar might not be perfect, but they will be making conversation in English and they will be motivated. Let the material find its own level. Prompt, cajole and tease the ideas from your students if they are reticent. Be positive but don't expect too much too soon.

- **Silence.** A little silence on your part can work wonders. Say something and wait. Wait long enough and you will always get a response. Try to involve everyone. Ask who prefers to be called on first and who last. Let the class feel you have your fingers firmly on their pulse. And if your situation allows it, give the students the freedom to move round the class, sit or stand, go outside for a breath of fresh air, a drink or even a cigarette!

7 Materials

- **Adapt to suit your circumstances.** Make your materials more or less elaborate as you require. Rely on common sense. If cards are called for, slips of paper can almost certainly be used. If it is difficult to obtain photocopies of the worksheets, in many cases the students can easily make a rough copy themselves.

- **Make up your own worksheets.** A series of points to be discussed during an activity may be turned into worksheets and handed out. Lists of discussion points can invariably be elicited from the students, too. It is not difficult to avoid presenting an activity lifelessly from the front. Moreover, the students can add interesting discussion points of their own to any of the lists and they should even be encouraged to write their ideas on the board wherever appropriate.

- **Visuals.** If pictures are to be used, they can be presented in a number of different ways: drawn on the board; on the overhead projector; on cardboard; photocopies, posters and so on.

- **Audio and video recordings** of the students can be used for many of the of activities. This is not mentioned over and over again.

8 Learning to learn

- **Learning skills.** At the end of each section there is a spread devoted to learner training. The activities here focus on study skills and include a number of ideas to help students learn effectively and reflect on the personal process of learning a foreign language.

- **Revision.** The problem with learning a language is said to be not remembering it but forgetting it and a number of the activities suggest ways of making revision easier and more fun. Revision should be an on-going process, whether there is an examination on the horizon or not. You don't have to carve the words you want to learn into your desk-top or write them on the wall but you might want to consider making notes on a bookmark, pasting notes around the house or writing vocabulary on your hands.

9 Beyond the classroom

The primary aims of *Creating Conversation in Class* are to stimulate students to talk about subjects that interest them in the classroom and give them the confidence to do so. The underlying aim is to encourage them to talk more English outside the confines of their lessons in everyday situations.

- **When the class is over.** I like to suggest that students continue their conversations even when the class is over. After a particularly effective lesson, this might actually happen spontaneously. You can also stimulate it as a homework activity, in which students work together on their English. The task set may be something as simple as telling them to repeat a topic they discussed with one student, after class with another. Thus the conversation initially created in class can be taken one step further.

- **Writing.** Topics discussed in class can become writing activities as homework. For example, tell your students to write a paragraph about the topic or prepare a brief summary of the points they discussed with their partners. Many students enjoy this sort of written consolidation and benefit greatly from it.

- **The Internet.** A large number of the activities can be done with a partner via the Internet. If you want to know where to start, *Making Connections* (page 66) is ideal. But it is possible to develop almost all the activities involving pairwork further in this way. Tell students who have access to the Internet to contact someone they know, someone whose English is at least at the same level as theirs, and do the activity on-line with them. It will motivate very many of your students to continue 'speaking' English to each other after class.

Although not all students have access to the Internet, it is well worth encouraging those who do to use it to improve their English. Other students can arrange to do the activities on the phone. And given the speed at which things are progressing, those who do have access will very probably soon outnumber those who don't.

10 Conclusion

Please think carefully about all the details of the instructions. They are only guidelines. Improvise and be resourceful. You will want to adapt the activities to your teaching situation. Open yourself to your classes and a new world of student interest and involvement will in turn reveal itself to you.

1

Getting Started

What do you do when you enter a classroom and start your lesson? The first couple of minutes of your lesson are critical in establishing rapport with the class. Why not surprise your students and broaden the range of what you do when you walk into the room? If this period that the students are settling down both physically and mentally, is carefully handled, you can facilitate a lot of learning without even realising it.

You might well start your lessons in some of the ways mentioned in this section: asking your students unusual questions; taking something into the class to prepare the way for the topic you will be discussing; saying or doing something that will surprise them; or even not saying anything at all. Here are sixty suggestions for getting started.

20 Starters

Twenty sample ways to start your class.

- Greet the students individually, ask them how they are feeling and coax a little small talk from them.

- Ask if the students can remember what you did in the last lesson.

- Check if the students can remember a specific teaching point from a previous lesson.

- Set a riddle.

- Do something completely unexpected.

- Say something provocative and controversial.

- Comment on some aspect of the students' appearance.

- Tease somebody about something.

- Get the students to report back on their homework.

- Ask each student for an example of something positive and something not so positive from their life.

- Tell some good news and some bad news from your life and ask the students to do the same.

- Take up some conversation points you recently discussed in class.

- Question the students on what they think about some topical issue.

- Ask the students to describe an aspect of their culture.

- Get the students to explain something to you.

- Request advice about something.

- Get the students to each ask you a question or two.

- Start your lesson with a short silence, a meditation or a prayer.

- Praise individual students or the whole class on their progress.

- Just stand or sit silently in front of the class and wait for a response.

Additional ideas

20 Questions

Twenty questions to get your students talking.

- What were you talking about when I came into the room?

- What did you do in your previous lesson?

- What did you do last night?

- What are your plans for this evening / the coming weekend / the holidays?

- What have you been reading recently?

- What's in the news today?

- Has anyone read their horoscope this week?

- Why is it so quiet / busy in town today?

- What's new at home / school / work or in general?

- When did you last use your English?

- Has anyone seen / heard the weather forecast?

- I think my watch is wrong. What's the exact time?

- What did you have for breakfast this morning?

- I've just bought a new ... What was the last thing you bought?

- At the last lesson you predicted the lottery result. Did you have any numbers correct?

- Last week we each guessed the score in the Cup Final. Did anyone get it right?

- I read / saw / heard yesterday that ... What do you think?

- Did anyone see that programme about ... on TV last night? What did you think of it?

- Is anyone missing? When was the last time he / she was here?

- What would you like to do today?

Additional ideas

20 Lead-ins

Twenty lead-ins to your main activity.

- Bring in a picture.

- Show a video clip.

- Tell an anecdote or story.

- Tell a joke.

- Play or sing a song.

- Read, or ask a student to read out, a short text on a related topic.

- Begin with a quotation or proverb.

- Ask a rhetorical question.

- Draw something indistinctly on the board and get the students to guess what it is.

- Play a tape or CD of some snippets of information connected with the topic.

- Mime the topic or some details connected with it.

- Brainstorm associated words and concepts.

- Make the topic the subject of a quick '20 Questions' session.

- Revise structures and vocabulary you expect to come up.

- Get the students to guess what the topic is from a list of key expressions associated with it.

- Tell the students what you plan to do today, and tell them why.

- Give each student a card with a word related to the topic written on it. Tell the students that they have two minutes to think about their words in silence. They then have to share their ideas and associations with the class.

- Tease the students by telling them you have a topic which is far too sophisticated for them, something you could never possibly do with them in class ... and then go on to do it when you've captured their interest.

- Tell the students you dreamed their English was perfect. Spend a few moments imagining what that would be like. Tell them you also dreamed what you were going to do today.

- As a simple guessing game, demonstrate what you are going to do today, without actually saying what it is.

Additional ideas

REFLECTING ON LEARNING

How Do You Learn?

Level: Intermediate
Time: 15 minutes
Language Functions: Reporting and comparing
Materials: An overhead projector, with transparencies and pens, or large cards and thick felt-tipped pens

Before Class

Write some sets of eight to ten numbers and letters clearly on transparencies or large cards

In Class

1 Tell the class you want to try a little experiment with them. Tell them you will **show** them a set of mixed numbers and letters for thirty seconds. Their task is to look at the set carefully and then try to recall the characters in the correct sequence. At this stage they should only **look** and should try not to repeat the characters aloud. They may not write anything down yet.

2 The first set might be: 7 L J 5 3 S D L 2 X. Be careful not to include characters like 'O', which could be either a number or a letter. Show the set on the card or overhead projector for thirty seconds and then ask the students to write down as much of it (in order) as they can recall.

3 Tell the students you will **read** the next set to them. Again their task is to recall the ten characters in sequence, without writing yet.

4 The second set could be: E 7 R W T 3 8 5 B P. Read the set out slowly and clearly. Read at even speed, with even intonation and with equal pauses between each character, i.e. **not** E7R WT 385 BP. Read the list three times and then ask the students to write down what they can remember. Abandon the 'no writing' rule between the second and third reading if students are struggling, although they should not simply write the characters down as in a dictation.

5 Tell the students to work individually and write down their own set of ten mixed numbers and letters.

6 Now get them to work in pairs, A and B. A traces his set in capital letters on the back of B's hand with a finger. A may do this up to three times. He may also interrupt the sequence to repeat a character if requested, and make a few appropriate comments such as 'Now we're coming to the last but one'. B should only now write down the list. Then it is B's turn to write her set on the back of A's hand in the same way. A and B should then check how well they got on.

7 In pairs, or as a class, get the students to discuss how well they were able to recall the three sets of numbers. Who did better visually, that is with the first set? Who did better auditorily, with the second set? Who found the last set, which were presented kinaesthetically, the easiest?

8 Say that you will now conclude the experiment by presenting a final set of ten characters. Explain that you will write the characters on the board and will also read them out loud. The students should try to recall the list a) visually b) auditorily and c) kinaesthetically. Explain that this means:

a They should look at the list carefully themselves. You will read out the list once and they will have a total of thirty seconds to study it.

b In addition, they should say the numbers and letters to themselves as often as they like.

c Finally, they should write the characters on the back of their own hands with a finger.

When you have done the experiment, check how well the students could recall the characters.

REFLECTING ON LEARNING

9 Finish off with a discussion of the most effective way to learn. What sort of learners are the students? Did the 'combined approach' improve their recall? What have they learned about themselves as learners? What is the best way to learn for each individual student? What strategies or mnemonics (memory aids) can one use? For example:

- Form a clear visual image of the material you are trying to recall.
- 'Chunk' the material wherever possible: in other words, learning sets of two or three characters is generally easier than trying to learn them in isolation.
- Make mental associations to jog your memory.

NOTE: I learned the basic idea behind this activity from Robert Dilts at a workshop on Neuro-Linguistic Programming (NLP).

Learning Skills

Level: Intermediate
Time: 30 minutes
Language Functions: Recalling the past; making recommendations
Materials: None

In Class

1 Tell your students to list about a dozen things they have learned to do in their lives. For example, learning to:

walk	bake
talk	do woodwork
read	ride a bike
write	use a computer
do sums	play tennis
play the guitar	drive

2 Now tell them to work in pairs and discuss these skills. They can include any relevant anecdotes and may discuss whatever aspects of the skills they wish. Which did they master easily and which caused them difficulty? Stress, however, that one aspect you would like them to pay particular attention to is the way they learned the skill in question.

3 Tell the students to continue by discussing the way they go about learning English. How does this compare with the way they mastered the other skills? Which learning strategies that worked for other skills might they be able to apply to learning English, whether to the whole subject or only a part of it?

Explain that the aim is to look for personal learning strategies which have proved effective in one area and see whether they can be transferred to another. For example:

- Nick says that he learned to use a computer relatively easily because he experimented a lot and wasn't scared of making mistakes. He suddenly realises that it is his fear of making mistakes in speaking English that is holding him back.

- Julie says her father taught her how to do woodwork. She always asked him when she had a question. She says that with English she tends to try and puzzle it out for herself and doesn't ask, even if she's hopelessly lost.

2

Breaking the Ice

This section contains activities for warming the students up and encouraging them to start talking to each other, losing their inhibitions and using English as the vehicle for classroom communication. Some activities are intended for students who have not been in the same class before. Others are intended for groups returning after a holiday or similar period when they have not been together.

The icebreaking stage should never be overlooked if you want your students to develop a sound basis for constructive conversation. When students get to know each other better, it helps them to relax and work efficiently, and while they are getting acquainted they are already speaking in English.

May I Introduce Myself?

Level
> Intermediate

Time
> 60-90 minutes

Language Functions
> Disclosing personal information; asking and answering questions

Materials
> Large sheets of paper and thick felt-tipped pens if you choose the last two options in Step 2

In Class

1 Tell the students you want to offer them an unusual way to introduce themselves to the class. You are going to let them choose the way they introduce themselves individually.

2 Ask them which 'icebreakers' (activities for introducing themselves) they know or have used in other courses or other situations. Can anyone think of any new, unusual icebreakers? Write them up on the board as prompts. If necessary, add a few of your own activities to the students' list.

A few well-known group icebreakers are:

- Simply introduce yourself to the class.

- Introduce yourself to the class but include some inaccuracies. The class has to try to distinguish fact from fiction.

- Interview another student about him / herself and report what you discovered to the whole class.

- Interview another student and report what you discovered, as if you were that student.

- In pairs, mime some significant details about your life to your partner, who then introduces you to the others.

- Draw three symbols from your life on a large sheet of paper and then use the drawing as the basis of your introduction.

- Draw a large sketch of aspects of your life and present it to the class.

3 Give the students about fifteen minutes to decide what they want to do and prepare their introductions. Then allow them five minutes each to introduce themselves and answer any questions they may be asked.

4 Tell them to work in pairs. Those who have already worked with a partner should choose someone else. Their task is now to choose another of the forms of introduction listed in Step 2 and work through it together. This time it does not have to be presented to the whole class but just to their partner.

Personal and Professional

Level

Intermediate

Time

30 minutes

Language Functions

Reporting; asking and answering questions in different tenses

Materials

Copies of the worksheet

In Class

1 Hand out copies of the worksheet and tell the students to use them to make notes about themselves. Explain that the aim of the activity is to talk about the details they fill in. Tell them they may supplement their notes with simple drawings, or even use small drawings without any words at all, if they prefer. Give a couple of examples of your own:

Personal past:

Tennis match I played last week

Personal present:

Spring – looking forward to doing the garden

Professional future:

New class next month – hope I get on with my students

2 If necessary, explain that 'personal' should not refer to intimate aspects of their private lives. Moreover, they need not find examples for every box on the grid, although they should find at least one example each of 'past', 'present' and 'future' so that they can practise the tenses.

3 Divide the class into pairs and tell the students to discuss the details they have filled in. They should ask each other questions and should pay attention to the tenses they use. Circulate, helping where necessary and noting any weaknesses, particularly in their use of the tenses, for remedial work.

NOTE: In the case of younger students to whom 'Personal and Professional' does not apply, you can modify the activity to refer to 'At Home and Not at Home' or 'At School and Not at School'.

	Personal	**Professional**
Past		
Present		
Future		

Creating Conversation in Class © Chris Sion published by DELTA PUBLISHING

Getting to Know You

Level

Intermediate

Time

30-45 minutes

Language Functions

Sharing and comparing personal information; taking notes

Materials

Copies of the worksheet

In Class

1 Divide the class into groups of about four students and give each student a copy of the worksheet. The worksheet is designed for groups of up to six students.

2 Tell your students to fill in their own names and the names of the others in their group in the 'Name' column.

3 Now tell them their task is to think of interesting and amusing things to talk about. These should be written at the top of each column. Each group must find examples of items to talk about in all the columns. So in addition to standard information about where they come from (their jobs, hobbies and whether they're married), they should include some more unusual items. For example: sign of the zodiac; lucky number; first English lesson; toothpaste; first cigarette; domestic pets and so on.

4 When the groups have settled on their items the students should fill in their grids individually. They should write their own examples next to their names in the appropriate columns in note form: no more than a couple of words are required for each example.

5 The students talk to each other about the items on their worksheets. They may fill in the worksheet by taking brief notes about each other if they wish. Once again, only a couple of words are required for each point, as the primary aim of the activity is speaking. However, the notes might prove very useful in Step 6.

6 Bring the groups together for a whole-class discussion. Ask one member of each group to report back on the items chosen by the group. Let each student report back on the most interesting point that emerged from their discussions.

Items → / Names ↓						

Creating Conversation in Class © Chris Sion published by DELTA PUBLISHING

Myself from A-Z

Level
Intermediate

Time
Several sessions of 15-30 minutes

Language Functions
Presenting information; asking and answering questions

Materials
Copies of the worksheet

Before Class
Prepare an A-Z of your own life as described in Step 1.

In Class

1 Tell the students you are going to spend the next few lessons on a project to give them the chance to talk about themselves. The basis of the exercise is for each student to talk about an aspect of their life connected with each of the letters of the alphabet. The aspects they come up with may be trivial, personal or humorous. Start with the A-Z of your own life, or give a few examples to clarify exactly what you want:

A *A is for ambulance because I am a voluntary ambulance driver at weekends.*

B *B is for baby because my wife is expecting a baby.*

C *C is for Cora, my first girlfriend and I'm not going to say anything about her.*

D *D is for diet. I'm trying to lose weight.*

E *E is for energy. I've just been on holiday and I'm feeling really fit.*

2 Give each student a copy of the worksheet and give them time to prepare their A-Z's. This is probably best started in class and completed as homework.

3 Make a timetable so the students know when it is their time to present.

4 The students present themselves at the arranged times. Be sure to allow question time for each contribution. It is important to strike a good balance between letting the speakers present their A-Z's and answer questions, without letting the activity going on too long.

NOTE: Tell the students to simply leave out the letters they find difficult, but encourage them not to give up too easily. Let them see how many letters they can incorporate. You can also easily shorten the activity by asking the students to restrict themselves to a given number of letters, say twelve or fifteen.

Other variations of this activity are to do an A-Z of your job or one of your hobbies. You could also do an A-Z of your friends or your family: not just their names, but focusing on interesting details about them.

A	
B	
C	
D	
E	
F	
G	
H	
I	
J	
K	
L	
M	
N	
O	
P	
Q	
R	
S	
T	
U	
V	
W	
X	
Y	
Z	

Creating Conversation in Class © Chris Sion published by DELTA PUBLISHING

Hands Up!

Level

Intermediate

Time

10 minutes + 20 minutes later in the lesson

Language Functions

Asking questions; exchanging and comparing personal information

Materials

None

Before Class

Make a list of ten questions about yourself which you would answer in the affirmative. The aim is to establish some common ground between you and your students, so the questions should be suitably geared to yourself and the type of students you expect to be teaching. For example:

- Who has never been in this building before?

- Who is right-handed?

- Who was born in Europe?

- Who is a vegetarian?

- Who went to bed after midnight last night?

- Who has a mobile phone?

- Who enjoys working in the garden?

- Who plays tennis?

- Who likes 'zapping' with the TV remote control?

- Who was born in the winter?

In Class

1 Tell the students that you want to get to know them and at the same time want to give them the chance of getting to know you. Explain that you are going to read out some questions that you yourself would answer 'Yes' to. Ask the students to raise their hands if their answers are also 'Yes'.

2 Read out the questions one by one. Ask the students to clarify their responses and offer a few of your own comments but keep the discussion brief at this stage. Observe the students closely, paying careful attention to their reactions. Eye contact is very important in ensuring that the students' responses are recognised. Pay attention to the reactions of all the students, even those who don't raise their hands.

3 Tell the students each to think of one question about themselves to which they would answer affirmatively.

4 Students take turns to read out their questions while the other class members, including you, raise their hands where applicable.

5 This step may be done either immediately or at a later stage in the lesson. Ask the students to recall the questions asked in Step 2 and Step 4. Write a list of the questions up on the board. Tell the students to work in pairs and discuss whichever points they find interesting. Now is the chance for them to talk in more detail and develop conversation.

NOTE: My favourite final question is 'Who has not yet put up their hand?' This ensures that everyone has at least one opportunity to participate.

Together Again

Level
    Intermediate

Time
    30-45 minutes

Language Functions
    Describing; narrating; reporting personal
    information

Materials
    None

In Class

1 If possible, sit with your students in a circle.
Explain that their task is simply to tell you
something about each member of the group. Tell
the students to keep their contributions short and,
wherever possible, to avoid repetition. Leave it
up to them to decide what they report on, only
prompting and helping them where it is
absolutely necessary.

A typical contribution might be:

'Anna's feeling great because she's just bought a
car; Peter is going back home next week; Joe
wants to become a vet; Mary likes hamburgers -
with lots of ketchup; David loves opera; Zoë likes
hard rock; Wilma went to California last year;
Eva's English is the best in the class and so on.

2 For convenience, work clockwise, starting with
the student on your left. Encourage a good
mixture of responses. Listen carefully to what the
students say about each other and pay attention
to the way in which the comments are made.
You can ask for brief explanations but you should
not try to develop conversations at this stage.

3 Tell the students that it's your turn now. Go round
the class making simple observations about the
way the students made their comments and
about what you learned about them.

4 Ask them to comment briefly on their classmates'
comments and your impressions.

5 Have one 'last round', this time allowing each
student to ask you one question about yourself.
Don't make your answers too long, either!

NOTE: This activity differs from the other icebreakers
in that it is only suitable for students who already
know each other. It is best used either when students
return after a holiday or similar break, or if you find
yourself an outsider in a class you have taken over
from another teacher. However, you may want to
include yourself, even though you are a stranger to
the group. You might learn something about your
reputation!

The Holidays

Level
Elementary

Time
20-30 minutes

Language Functions
Narrating and describing; talking about the past

Materials
Copies of the worksheet

In Class

1 Welcome your students back after the holidays and tell them to think over what they did since they were last together. What were the best and the worst moments?

2 Give each student a copy of the worksheet and ask them to each choose a pair of concepts to be written in the spaces at the top of the empty columns of their grids. For example, you could write up this list on the board:

- At home / Away

- Alone / Together

- Indoors / Outdoors

- Fun / Boring

- Important / Not important

- Expensive / Cheap

3 The students should now write the pair of concepts they have chosen in the spaces at the top of the grid and then fill it in appropriately. Key words and notes are sufficient. It is not necessary to write full sentences.

4 Divide the class into pairs and tell them they have ten or fifteen minutes to talk about the information on their grids.

5 If they get through the material quickly, tell them to repeat Step 3 and Step 4 with other items from the list.

The Holidays		
Concepts →		
The Beginning		
The Middle		
The End		

TURNING NEGATIVE TO POSITIVE

Refusing to Learn

Level: Intermediate
Time: 30 minutes
Language Functions: Making suggestions; describing; making resolutions
Materials: None

In Class

1 Tell the students to think of everything they could do to make their learning less effective and write their ideas up on the board. For example:

- not listening in class
- not doing the homework
- constantly translating into the mother tongue
- not asking for help when they don't understand
- never looking through their notes
- never contributing in class (not even internally)
- writing everything down
- never writing anything down
- looking everything up in the dictionary
- not looking anything up in the dictionary
- 'switching off'
- cultivating a thoroughly negative attitude

2 Tell the students to work in pairs and discuss which of the points on the board they are most guilty of themselves.

3 Tell them to choose one or two points to try and improve on. Tell them to think about it carefully and make a clear resolution to change. Merely paying 'lip service' to a good idea will not help them at all. If a student is willing, their partner can be given the task of checking up on them over a period of time, not by carrying a big stick but rather as a 'buddy' offering friendly support.

Effective Learning

Level: Intermediate
Time: 30 minutes + 15 minutes in a later lesson
Language Functions: Reflecting; making recommendations; comparing
Materials: Copies of the worksheet

In Class

1 Tell your students you want them to think about how they learn and about how they could learn more effectively. What could they do to improve their learning skills? Ask them to begin by saying whatever ideas they freely associate with effective learning. For example: asking when you don't understand; not trying to translate every single word; having clear goals; motivation; positive thinking; taking frequent breaks; repeating and checking new vocabulary regularly; trying to find peace and quiet; setting aside some time for English every day and so on. Be sure to elicit the ideas from the students. Don't be tempted to give them all the answers yourself.

2 Give out the worksheets. Tell the students to discuss them in pairs and then report back on the one or two most significant points in their discussion. Build up a list of effective learning strategies on the board.

3 Ask the students at a subsequent lesson whether they have changed their learning habits and what progress they feel they are making as a result of their new approach. Discuss these points with them. For example:

- What have you tried?
- How successful have you been?
- How much time did you need?
- How do you feel about your improvement?
- What is the next step for you?

Discuss these questions with a partner. Be prepared to tell the class the most significant points in your discussion. You should also make some clear decisions about improving your learning strategies, as you will be expected to report to the class on your progress at a later lesson.

- What exactly do you do in order to you learn?

- What do you see, hear and feel when you're learning?

- When you're trying to learn something, do you approach it positively, feeling confident you can do it, or do you wonder about your ability?

- What do you remember of what you learned last week / last term / last year / when you went to school?

- What have you learned since you left school?

- What have you learned about how you learn best?

- How **do** you learn best?

- Is there a difference between the way you learn English and the way you have tried to learn other subjects?

- What could you do to improve your learning effectiveness?

- What strategies could you use? This applies both to strategies you are already using in other areas and to those you could learn from other people.

- How could you go about translating theory into practice?
  In other words, how exactly could you integrate these strategies into your learning behaviours?

- What new strategies would you like to try?

- Do you know the saying 'The road to hell is paved with good intentions'?
  What does it mean? What do you really agree to do? Give it to yourself
  in writing and display it in a prominent place where you can see it.

Creating Conversation in Class © Chris Sion published by DELTA PUBLISHING

3

Talking to Each Other

This section contains a miscellany of topics to keep your students talking once the class has been formed and the ice broken. Everyone has something interesting to say, whether it is expressing an opinion, exchanging information, answering questions or giving advice.

Here is a wide variety of activities united by a single aim: to continue stimulating your students to keep talking in English as often as they can.

More Equal Than Others

Level
Intermediate

Time
30-45 minutes

Language Functions
Comparing; describing

Materials
None

In Class

1 Discuss with the class the fact that not all adjectives can be compared. For example, we can compare something 'big' with something else which is 'bigger', or someone who is 'intelligent' with someone else who is 'more intelligent'. However, if we are talking about something which is 'perfect' or 'impossible', we cannot say that something else is 'more perfect' or 'more impossible', except as a joke.

2 Start a list of adjectives on the board and elicit additional examples from the students until you have a good selection of adjectives:

attractive	meaningless
absolute	fair
superior	sufficient
universal	catastrophic
different	tolerant
obvious	neurotic
absurd	pregnant
emotional	unique
musical	normal
clear	exact
still	correct
aggressive	accurate
equal	polite

It is important to have a list containing a fair mixture of adjectives which can and cannot be compared. Make sure the meanings are clear.

3 Tell the students to work in small groups and discuss which of the adjectives can and cannot be compared. Some students will inevitably interpret the adjectives strictly, others loosely, which can generate a great deal of discussion. Encourage the students to think of several situations in which the adjectives can be used. For example, in the case of 'clear', we can have: a clear explanation; a clear day; clear water; a clear conscience; a clear victory; a clear sound; a clear image and so on.

4 Ask the groups to report back on examples where they were not all in agreement.

5 Now that students have gathered a lot more words to express themselves with, divide them into pairs and tell them to discuss:

a Which of the adjectives on the list most / least apply to themselves. Why?

b Which other adjectives, not on the list, best describe themselves. Why?

c Which adjectives they find useful and could imagine themselves using in their conversations. Why?

Time to Talk

Level

Intermediate

Time

45 minutes

Language Functions

Exchanging and comparing information and opinions; describing

Materials

Copies of the worksheet

3 Finish off with a whole class discussion about which topics the students are most interested in and which they have the most difficulty with. This can be useful for planning future conversation classes.

NOTE: Some students might find the worksheet quite difficult to fill in. It requires a fair amount of reflection. Rather than spending too much time on this, you could start it in class and ask students to complete it for homework for a discussion in the following lesson.

In Class

1 Ask your students what they talk about outside the classroom. Who do they talk to? Who do they most like talking to? Collect a few responses from around the class and then give out the worksheets.

2 Tell them to fill in the worksheet individually and then discuss it with a partner. They should use their lists to tell their partner: what they talk about and who with; what they say; which people they most like talking to, and why. They can also include further details, such as when and where their conversations usually take place. The list of subjects might include:

pop groups	sport
cinema	work
shopping	eating out
children	news
parents	TV
homework	gardening
religion	books
weather	friends
the Internet	computer games
brothers and sisters	home

Subject	People you talk to about it	Further details

Ask Me a Question

Level

    Intermediate

Time

    60-90 minutes

Language Functions

    Asking and answering questions;
    exchanging information

Materials

    Copies of the worksheet; an overhead
    projector is useful but not essential

Name	Topic	Question
Bill	Internet	Do you ever use the Internet to help you with your homework?
Anna	Sumo wrestling	What do you think about Sumo for women?
Joey	Holidays in Scotland	Can you recommend a good youth hostel in the Highlands?

In Class

1 Hand out copies of the worksheet. Fill in the students' names on your copy of the worksheet and tell them to do the same.

2 Explain that you want to give them the chance to talk about something that they really know something about. Each student should give you one topic which they feel they could answer questions about. Give them a chance to think of something suitable which will generate lots of questions. Each student should call out their topic. Tell all the students to write their classmates' topics on their worksheet next to their name.

3 Each student has to write one question about each topic on their worksheets. The questions can be written out in full or in note form. Give a few examples yourself so that the task is clear and offer help where necessary.

4 When they have finished writing down their questions, the students should mingle and ask each other the questions they have written about each topic. Stress that the questions are intended as starting points, springboards to further conversation. They should try and speak to as many of their classmates as they can.

Name	Topic	Question

Creating Conversation in Class © Chris Sion published by DELTA PUBLISHING

Collecting Key Words

Level

Intermediate

Time

45 minutes

Language Functions

Comparing

Materials

Dictionaries are useful but not essential

Before Class

Decide on a topic you want to discuss and prepare a set of about twelve words or expressions relating to it.

In Class

1 Tell your students the topic you want to discuss. It might be related to the news, be of local interest or be something linked to a text or video, or anything else covered recently in class. They may use dictionaries if they wish.

2 Divide them into pairs and ask them to think of about twelve words or expressions connected with the topic. Give them five to ten minutes to do this.

3 Explain that you have also prepared some key words and expressions relating to the topic and that you want to compare their examples with your own.

4 Ask the pairs one by one to provide a couple of examples at a time, to be written up on the board. Take your turn, adding your own examples. If words come up more than once, just put a mark next to them for each occurrence. It is better not to ask a group to give all their examples at once, as they might decide that they have finished their contribution, and 'switch off'.

5 In pairs or small groups, the students should now discuss the topic, using as many of the words and expressions on the board as they can.

Topics from A-Z

Level
Elementary

Time
30-45 minutes

Language Functions
Asking and answering questions; disclosing information; agreeing and disagreeing

Materials
None

In Class

1 Write the alphabet on the board in large, clear letters. Tell the students to think of a couple of words beginning with each letter of the alphabet.

2 Go round the class asking for one contribution from each student. It is not necessary to work systematically. As the activity is built up, the board might look something like this:

3 Tell the students to work in pairs. Explain that a selection of these words will form the basis of their discussion. Tell the students to pick between five and ten words from the list that they would like to talk about. They should agree on which words they both find interesting. They may make minor modifications or interpretations if they wish. For example, 'Europe' could be taken to be 'the continent of Europe' or 'the European Community'. 'Jealous' could be modified to 'jealousy'. The important point is that they agree on the subjects.

4 Give the pairs a certain amount of time to talk and leave them to it, simply being on hand to help when needed.

NOTE: You can easily make the activity more specific by including a qualification in Step 3. For example, pick five to ten words that are connected with school, your job, last weekend, the Christmas holidays and so on. You could also use the worksheet on page 29 and get students to complete it for homework as the basis for discussion in the next class.

A		N	*never*
B	*book*	O	
C		P	
D		Q	
E	*Europe*	R	
F		S	*soccer, sunshine, smile*
G		T	*tennis*
H	*holiday, home, happiness*	U	
I		V	
J	*job, jealous*	W	*winter*
K	*kaleidoscope*	X	
L		Y	
M		Z	*zoo*

Past, Present, Future

<table>
<tr><td>Level
Intermediate

Time
30-60 minutes

Language Functions
Asking and answering questions in different tenses

Materials
Copies of the worksheet</td></tr>
</table>

In Class

1 Tell the students to prepare three questions individually to ask each other. The questions may be about any subject at all. The only restriction is that one question should relate to the present, one to the past and one to the future and that the questions should be suitable starting points for making conversation. 'What colour is your sweater?' would not generate much to say.

2 Draw three columns on the board and label them **Past**, **Present** and **Future**. Write up a selection of the students' questions on the board in the relevant column like this:

Modify the questions if necessary to make them more suitable for conversation and briefly revise points of grammar as you go. Try to include at least one question from each student. You should also make sure that past, present and future are more or less equally represented.

Explain why you choose to put the questions in the various columns if it is not clear, for example, that 'What are you doing this weekend?' is a question about the future although the form is present continuous. 'Have you seen *Hamlet*?' could go in the Present or Past column. Hand out copies of the worksheet and get students to write down the questions.

3 Tell the students to work in pairs and spend ten minutes asking each other questions about the past from their worksheets. They should then change partners and ask each other the questions about the present, again for about ten minutes. They then get a further ten minutes to change partners once more and ask each other the questions about the future. Stress that the questions should be seen as conversation openings and that one-word answers are not acceptable.

Past	Present	Future
Where were you when the Berlin Wall was torn down?	*What do you think should be done to combat drug addiction?*	*Who do you think will be the next President of the United States?*
Where were you born?	*What sort of house or flat do you live in?*	*Where would you like to go on holiday next year?*
What sort of school did you go to?	*Who is your favourite teacher?*	*What will you look like in ten years' time?*
What books did you use to like as a child?	*How often do you go to parties?*	*What are you doing this weekend?*

Past	Present	Future

Creating Conversation in Class © Chris Sion published by DELTA PUBLISHING

Waste Not, Want Not

Level
    Intermediate

Time
    30 minutes

Language Functions
    Asking and answering questions; reporting;
    comparing and describing

Materials
    Copies of the worksheet

In Class

1 Write **Waste Not, Want Not** on the board. Tell
the students you want to discuss how thrifty they
are. Check that they know what thrift is and
explain if they don't. Ask if the implications of
thrift have changed over recent years. Ask the
students if they can think of any examples of
frugality or even excessive thrift from their own
lives and whether they regard themselves as
thrifty people.

2 Hand out the worksheets and tell the students
first to read through the questions and tick 'yes'
or 'no' for each one.

3 Divide the class into pairs and ask them to
compare and explain their answers.

4 Ask the students to report back briefly on the
most interesting parts of their discussions.

NOTE: If your students come from a wide range of
different backgrounds, you should bear in mind that
what is an absurd degree of thrift for one student may
be almost a question of survival for another.

Read through the following questions and give yourself one point for every question to which you answer 'Yes'. Add up your score and compare with the analysis at the end of the worksheet.

When you are finished with the scoring, go on to discuss the questions with your partner. Use the items to develop conversation. Short answers are not enough.

	YES	NO
● Do you remove and keep the paperclips if you're going to throw away papers which are clipped together?	☐	☐
● Do you carefully remove wrapping paper from a gift so you can re-use it?	☐	☐
● Do you collect used sheets of A4 paper to use the clean side as scrap notepaper?	☐	☐
● Do you squash fragments of old soap onto the new bar you start using?	☐	☐
● Do you deliver letters to people living in your neighbourhood rather than posting them?	☐	☐
● Do you keep used nails and screws so you can use them again?	☐	☐
● Would you continue using a biro that was almost empty, but not quite?	☐	☐
● When vacuum cleaning the house, would you go out of your way to save a rubber band on the floor?	☐	☐
● Do you eat the last couple of slices of bread even if they're a bit dry?	☐	☐
● Do you usually try to get the last little bit of toothpaste out of the tube?	☐	☐
● Do you keep plastic bags to use them again?	☐	☐

Score

12-15 points: You are very thrifty and extremely careful not to waste anything.

8-11 points: Average. Quite thrifty but not excessively so.

5-7 points: Not very thrifty at all. Almost wasteful in some situations.

0-4 points: Definitely not thrifty at all. A life of waste!

Creating Conversation in Class © Chris Sion published by DELTA PUBLISHING

General Motors

Level
Intermediate

Time
30 minutes

Language Functions
Describing; comparing; giving personal information

Materials
None

In Class

1 As a lead-in to the topic, namely talking about cars, ask the class what sorts of numbers occur in describing cars. Build up the following list on the board:

number of doors	number of cylinders
horse power	petrol consumption
number of seats	capacity of engine
top speed	mileage
year	capacity of petrol tank
cruising speed	price

2 If the students are car owners, tell them to work in pairs and discuss their own cars with reference to the above points. If most students do not have cars, see the suggestions in the **Note** below.

3 Continue by asking the students to discuss a selection of the following points:

- Do you like travelling by car?

- Have you got a driving licence?

- How long have you had your car?

- When did you learn to drive?

- Who do you allow to drive your car?

- Are you satisfied with your car? Would you buy another of the same make?

- What does your car mean to you? Is it just a means of transport or do you have an almost personal relationship with it?

- How often do you:
    fill up with petrol?
    check the oil?
    check the tyres?
    have your car serviced?

4 Finish off with a discussion of some of the following points:

- What should be done about pollution from cars?

- Do you think there are too many cars on the road?

- Are cars a necessary evil?

- Can you imagine the car of the future?

NOTE: If few of the students in the class have cars, you could focus instead on the images used in car advertising: what ideas are associated with different types of cars; what a car says about a person and so on. Alternatively, you could ask them to discuss their parents' car or their dream car before moving on to the general discussion in Step 4.

Safety First

Level
Intermediate

Time
45 minutes

Language Functions
Giving advice

Materials
None

In Class

1 Tell the students you are going to divide the class into three groups for a discussion and that the subject you want to focus on is safety. Each group is to investigate a different aspect of safety.

2 Divide the class into the three groups as follows:

Group 1: Safety on the road
Group 2: Safety at work
Group 3: Safety in the home

3 Tell the groups to think of as many aspects of their subjects as they can, for example:

On the road:
Obey the speed limits. Drive particularly carefully when it is icy. Leave a safe distance between you and the car in front on the motorway.

At work:
No smoking in the laboratory. Wear a protective helmet on a building site. Don't wear loose clothes if you work with machinery.

In the home:
If you have young children don't cook on the front rings of the cooker. Install smoke alarms. Don't change a light bulb if your hands are wet.

If necessary, appoint one member of each group as a coordinator. Note that it is important that each member of the group should write down the examples, in preparation for Step 4.

4 When the groups have finished, tell the class to re-group in threes. These new groups should have one student from each of Groups 1, 2 and 3 working together. Their task is to report back on the various aspects of safety they discussed.

Further examples may be mentioned in the new groups and the discussion may continue for some time, either in the groups, as a whole class activity or both.

LEARNING TO REVISE

Tattoos

Level: Elementary
Time: 30 minutes
Language Function: Revising vocabulary
Materials: Ballpoint pens

In Class

1 Tell your students you want to spend some time revising vocabulary. Tell them to take a piece of paper and draw a line down the middle. One side is for a list of words they have recently learned and are sure about. The other is for a list of words they have been exposed to but which they are not yet sure about. Tell them they have about fifteen minutes to look through their books and notes and make their lists.

2 Tell them to compare with a partner the words they have listed as 'not yet sure about'.

3 Ask if anyone has any friends or acquaintances with a tattoo or if they have ever thought about having a tattoo themselves. Explain that the reason for your question is an amusing idea for vocabulary revision: that they should take a ballpoint pen and write a couple of words they want to learn on themselves like tattoos.

4 The students decide what words they want to tattoo themselves with and write or illustrate them clearly on their hands or wrists so that they can be seen, both by themselves and their classmates, for the rest of the day.

5 Finish off by asking the students to report on which words they selected and why.

6 Follow up the activity in the next lesson by asking the students if they can now remember the words they chose for their tattoos.

Streets Ahead

Level: Intermediate
Time: 30-40 minutes
Language Function: Recalling vocabulary
Materials: None

In Class

1 Ask the students to tell you about the area where they are living at present: local street names; shops; buildings; restaurants and so on.

2 Ask them to draw a simple map of where they spend most of their time. The map could be split into more than one part if necessary. For example: home and work or home and school. Tell them to include some street names and other details as mentioned in Step 1.

3 Get the students to look through their notes and books and pick out about a dozen useful words and expressions they want to revise. Give them about ten to fifteen minutes.

4 Now tell them to rename some of the streets, shops, buildings and so on, using the vocabulary they want to revise. For example:

Think-Thought-Thought Street
For Two Years Road
Sunrise Avenue
Improbable House
Most Beautiful Bank
Ugliest Supermarket

5 Divide the class into pairs or small groups and tell the students to present their maps to each other. Alternatively students could present their maps to the whole class, using a flip chart or overhead projector.

LEARNING TO REVISE

6 Tell the students that they should imagine themselves in the locations they have drawn and should say the 'revision names' of the places to themselves as they do so. The emphasis here is on consolidating vocabulary learned rather than creating conversation but this strategy provides invaluable fluency practice. Most important of all, next time they are actually in those places, they should repeat the new names they have given them, as a way of recalling the vocabulary out of the classroom. Tell the students you will ask them to report back at the next lesson.

Revised Identity Cards

Level: Intermediate
Time: 30 minutes
Language Function: Revising vocabulary
Materials: Pieces of thin card slightly bigger than a postcard

Before Class

You should prepare a list of words and expressions to revise with the class, unless you prefer to tell the students to select vocabulary to revise themselves

In Class

1 Write up on the board a list of words and expressions you want to revise, or tell the students to spend a few minutes looking through their books and notes and to pick out about a dozen vocabulary items they want to revise.

2 Tell them to make a list of the sort of information typically found on a passport or identity card, for example: name, maiden name, date and place of birth, address, occupation and so on.

3 Give each student a card. Say that this is their Revised Identity Card. They should fill it in, basing the information on their cards on the vocabulary they want to revise. They can also include any other amusing details to make the activity more lively. Introduce yourself first with your card so the students are clear about what you want. For example:

Name:	*Joe Sales Drive*
Address:	*27 Recipe Street, Economics Town*
Wife's (maiden) name:	*Janet Since a Point in Time*
Place of Birth:	*Rising Sun, Alabama*
Sign of the Zodiac:	*Indigestion*
Occupation:	*Photographer*
Hobby:	*Photography*

4 Tell the students to mingle and introduce themselves to each other in their revised identities. Insist that they should not just read out the information on their cards. They should say 'I was born in Rising Sun, Alabama' **not** 'Place of Birth: Rising Sun, Alabama'. You'll probably find that you won't need to tell them to explain vocabulary to anyone who doesn't understand it. They'll just do it naturally!

4

Talking About People

This section contains a collection of activities that are all connected in one way or another with talking about people. It begins with material centring on ways of describing people and concludes with a personality profile. The profile does not claim to be scientific but it is thought-provoking and will certainly give you something to talk about.

Students are given opportunities for discussion, ranging from commenting on the lives of famous people to talking about where they would like to sit. The activities aim to engage the students' interest through constant reference to their own lives and personal experience.

Prizes

Level
Intermediate

Time
45 minutes

Language Functions
Describing and comparing

Materials
None

In Class

1 Ask the students if they or any of their friends or families have ever won a prize. Give them time to tell you the details and answer questions about what happened.

2 Tell the students you want them to think of some prizes they could award themselves. Write a list of examples up on the board. Provide your own examples at first, adding whatever good ideas the students contribute. Tell them that any constructive ideas are welcome but that you do not want negative examples such as a prize for the dirtiest fingernails or for the student who makes the most mistakes. The sorts of prizes you could start with might be for the student who:

- has the highest standards
- is the best all-rounder
- is the most balanced
- is the most punctual
- is the keenest
- has the longest hair
- has made the most progress
- has missed the fewest lessons
- is the most helpful
- is the most independent
- has the most interesting ideas
- knows the most about computers

3 Divide the class into pairs and tell them to award a prize to every student in the class. They are not restricted to the list on the board. If they wish, they may specify what the prize is, for example a cup of coffee, a silver trophy or £100.

4 Ask the pairs to read out and if necessary explain their decisions. They should address the person who they want to give the prize to directly, as it is more personal to talk to the person concerned rather than making a statement about that person to the class. For example:

'Bob, we're giving you the prize for the most imaginative student in the group because you always have such good ideas and can express them so well.'

5 Now ask the students to say which prizes they appreciated, which prizes they would have liked to get and which prizes they would have awarded to themselves.

NOTE: This idea is intended for classes which have been together for some time and in which the students know each other quite well.

The People in Your Life

Level
   Intermediate

Time
   30-45 minutes

Language Functions
   Describing; evaluating

Materials
   Copies of worksheet

In Class

1 Tell the students to think of as many different ways of describing people as they can and write them up on the board. For example:

physical characteristics:
   tall, short, old, young, attractive, thin ...

personal characteristics:
   musical, friendly, sporting, grumpy, introverted ...

2 Tell the students you want them to talk about the people in their lives. Elicit some examples from the class:

close family	classmates
distant family	boss
neighbours	secretary
local shopkeepers	doctor
colleagues	dentist

3 Hand out a worksheet to each student and check that they understand it. Ask them to make a note of their answers. Then divide the class into pairs or small groups and tell them to discuss the questions on the worksheet.

Think about some people in your life and answer these questions.

- What do you like about them?

- What do you dislike about them?

- What do they look like?

- How would you describe their character?

- What sort of background are they from?

Now think about your first impressions of people and answer these questions.

- What do you tend to notice when you first meet people?

- What draws you to or turns you away from people?

- Are you tolerant of others' eccentricities?

- Are first impressions generally reliable?

- What first impression do you think you make?

- What first impression would you like to make?

- What would you like the people in your life to think or say about you?

Creating Conversation in Class © Chris Sion published by DELTA PUBLISHING

Theme for a Dream

Level

Intermediate

Time

30-45 minutes

Language Functions

Describing; making notes; expressing opinions; giving feedback; expressing wishes

Materials

Cassette recorder and relaxing, dreamlike, meditative music

Before Class

Prepare a dream sequence about how you would like the class to be. Choose the examples tactfully, thinking carefully about the students' personal needs. Nightmares and negative emotions are absolutely not appropriate in this activity.

In Class

1 Start by playing the music and telling the students just to relax and listen. Build the activity up slowly. After a while, tell them that you have had the most beautiful dream. Describe the context of the dream, paying attention to the landscape and other details and gradually letting the dream sequence unfold.

2 Continue by saying that the whole class was in the dream too. It was really good to see them there because:

- Maria was smiling. She had just received the letter she's been waiting for.

- Gerald was getting the tenses right without any problems.

- Bobby was speaking fluently, without hesitation.

- My voice wasn't hoarse and strained towards the end of the day.

Tell the class that you woke up with a really good feeling, as if your dream had come true.

3 Give the students a couple of minutes to reflect quietly on what you said. Let them express their feelings about it. Should students get defensive, reply that 'a dream is a dream'.

4 Tell them to make up dreams of their own, not necessarily about their classmates, but also about any aspect of their lives: homes; holidays; jobs and so on. Sweet dreams only, please! They need not write full sentences, notes are perfectly satisfactory.

5 Start the music again and let the students share their dreams in pairs, small groups or as a whole class.

NOTE: This activity is intended for classes which have been working together for some time and know each other well.

Show Me a Picture

Level
Elementary

Time
30 minutes + 30 minutes + several later sessions of 20-30 minutes if you use the video option

Language Functions
Talking about the past; asking and answering questions; presenting information; describing

Materials
If you do the video option, you need a video recorder and monitor

In Class

1 Divide the students into groups of about six and tell them their task is to talk about a picture they have at home. 'Picture' should be interpreted in its broadest sense, to include paintings, portraits, posters, photographs and so on. They should each describe their chosen picture, perhaps adding information about which room of the house it is in, where it comes from or any other interesting details.

2 Tell them that you want to go on talking about pictures in the next lesson. This time the material they are to use should be a photograph showing some aspect of their lives they would enjoy talking about. Ask them to bring a couple of interesting photographs to the next lesson. Make a special point at the end of the lesson of reminding them to bring the photos.

3 At the next lesson, divide the class once again into groups of six. The composition of the groups may be the same as before but need not be. Tell the students to take turns at showing their photos and asking each other questions about them.

Video option

1 Tell the class you would now like to follow up the work on pictures by using some video clips. Has anybody got suitable video material of their homes or hobbies or holidays that they would be able to bring to class? The video clips should be no longer than five minutes. The students should be prepared to talk about their videos but should restrict themselves to a maximum of five minutes for what they have to say, so there is enough time for questions. Make a timetable of who will show their video when and be sure to remind them at the lesson before. It's advisable to have one or two students 'on standby' at each lesson in case the presenter is absent.

2 The students show their videos at the scheduled times over the next few lessons. The other students make a note of their questions and ask them after the viewing or occasionally interrupt to ask their questions. The student presenting the video can also choose to stop the video sometimes to make a point or keep their comments till the end. It's often advisable to let the class see the videos more than once as this helps to generate more questions.

Short and Sweet

Level
Elementary

Time
10-20 minutes + later sessions of
10-20 minutes for each variation

Language Functions
Asking and answering questions;
exchanging information

Materials
None

In Class

1 Write some of the numbers connected with your life on the board. They can be any numbers at all. For example: house or flat number; telephone number; shoe size; weight; height; age; number of years you have lived at your present address; number of children; calories you allow yourself per day and so on.

2 Tell the students to guess what the numbers refer to. Prompt them in order to elicit the questions and keep the pace brisk.

3 Now it is the their turn. Tell them to each write down about ten numbers from their lives. They should then work in pairs and try to guess what the numbers refer to.

Variations
A: Dates
Do the activity as outlined above but instead of numbers do important dates, for example: birthdays in your family; date you left home; date you started work; date you met your spouse; a date that changed your life; the date you started or stopped smoking and so on.

B: Names
As above but this time using the first names of people who have played an important role in your life.

C: Abbreviations
Do the activity now using various different abbreviations reflecting aspects of your life. For example, in my own case:

CMHS - my initials; HCC Heerlen - Hockey and Cricket Club Heerlen, a local sports club; UCT - the University of Cape Town, where I studied when I lived in South Africa; PIN - my personal identification number, but I'm not saying what it is; and so on.

Famous People

Level
Intermediate

Time
30-45 minutes

Language Functions
Describing; evaluating

Materials
None

In Class

1 Tell the students to each write down the names of three famous people. They may be dead or alive but should be real people, not characters from fiction.

2 Ask each student to nominate one of the people they noted and build up a list on the board. If necessary, let the students briefly explain who the people they have nominated are. Not everybody may know them. Good examples would be:

Hillary Clinton	Vincent van Gogh
Joan of Arc	Tiger Woods
Sigmund Freud	Oprah Winfrey
Nelson Mandela	Queen Victoria
David Beckham	Albert Schweitzer
Elvis Presley	Socrates
Albert Einstein	Oscar Wilde
Beethoven	Pete Sampras
Margaret Thatcher	Venus Williams
Galileo	Mohammed Ali
Winston Churchill	Christopher Columbus

3 Divide the class into pairs and tell them to choose five of the famous people from the list to talk about. Write the following points on the board as prompts, and tell the students to discuss the people they have selected.

- What do you know about them?

- What do you admire or dislike about them and why?

- Which qualities of any of the famous people on the list would you most like to have?

- Would you like to be famous? If so, what would you like to be famous for?

- Have you ever met a famous person?

- Think of some questions you'd like to ask any of the people on the list. How do you think they would answer?

4 Set the following optional homework task: the students should look up a few of the names on the list in an English reference book. They should read up on them and briefly report back at the next lesson.

Spirals

Level
Elementary

Time
30 minutes + 30 minutes in a later lesson

Language Functions
Describing; comparing

Materials
Copies of the worksheet

In Class

1 Hand out a copy of the worksheet to each student and draw a large spiral on the board. Tell the students you want to use this as the basis of a conversation. Fill in the spiral by writing 'home' at the centre and then working outwards: 'street', 'neighbourhood', 'suburb', 'town', 'county', 'country'. Let the students modify the detail where necessary, for instance 'province' or 'state' might be apply rather than 'county', depending on where they live.

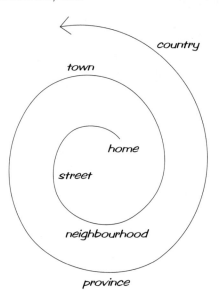

2 Tell the students their task is to discuss what's happening in these areas of their lives. What are the people in these places talking about? What are the issues on their minds at present? You can either leave the instruction quite open or give a selection of starting points for discussion, such as relating the subject to:

● something old / something new

● something pleasant / something not so pleasant

● something exciting / something boring

● something successful / something unsuccessful

● a beginning / an end

3 Follow up the activity by telling the students to prepare other spirals to talk about in the next lesson. For example:

For students in business:
desk, office, department, general department, division, subsidiary, company, global market place

For all students:
immediate family, grandparents, cousins, second cousins

In all cases you should encourage the students to modify the items in their spirals to make the activity match their lives as closely as possible.

Spirals

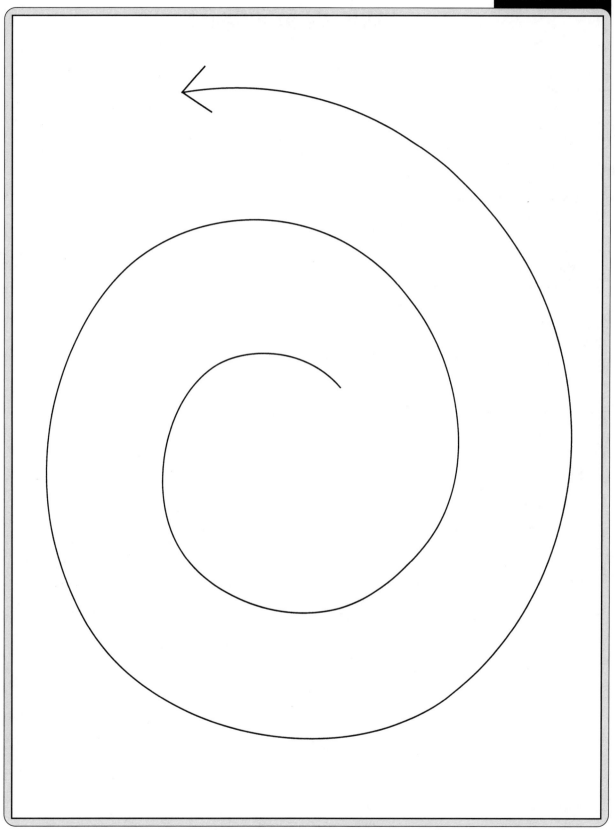

Creating Conversation in Class © Chris Sion published by DELTA PUBLISHING

What's in a Seat?

Level
Intermediate

Time
30 minutes

Language Functions
Reporting; expressing preferences;
describing position

Materials
Copies of the worksheet

In Class

1 Ask the students to close their eyes and try and
recall where their classmates are sitting. Then let
them open their eyes and discuss, either in pairs,
small groups or as a whole class, how well they
got on. How difficult was it?

2 The next question to discuss is why the students
are sitting where they are sitting. Do they have a
fixed place in the class? Why have they chosen
to sit at the back or the front or the side? How do
they feel if they can't sit where they want to?

3 Tell the students you want them to talk about
where they sit in different situations. Hand out
the worksheet and tell the students to discuss the
questions in pairs. Remind them that the object
of the exercise is to open up and then develop a
conversation and that one-word answers are not
acceptable.

4 Finish off the activity by asking the pairs to report
back to the whole class on anything of special
interest that came up in their conversations.

NOTE: This activity was inspired by Mario Rinvolucri.

Where do you usually sit? Discuss the following questions with your partner. Explain your answers.

- Where do you like to sit at the cinema / the theatre / a concert hall / the circus?

- Where do you sit on a bus / train / plane?

- Where do you sit at work?

- Where do you prefer to sit in a restaurant?

- What is your favourite seat in the living-room? Have you got a special place?

- Where did you use to sit as a child at school?

- Where do you like sitting in your English classes?

- Where do you like sitting in your other classes?

- Where do you usually sit at a lecture or formal presentation?

- Where is your place with your family at the table?

- Where did you use to sit at the table with your family as a child? Who decided where you sat?

- Are there any places where you regularly sit which you would like to change?

- Does it make any difference where you sit?

Creating Conversation in Class © Chris Sion published by DELTA PUBLISHING

Whistle While You Work

Level
Intermediate

Time
30-45 minutes

Language Functions
Reporting; asking and answering questions

Materials
Copies of the worksheet

In Class

1 To warm the class up, ask your students if they can pat their heads with one hand while they rub circles on their stomachs with the other. Let them try doing it.

2 After a couple of minutes, ask the students how many things they can do at the same time. Give them a couple of minutes to prepare and then let them report back. You might get examples such as: 'I can drive my car, eat a sweet, listen to music and talk to the passengers'. If these responses generate comments such as 'You should watch the road!' or 'You shouldn't talk with your mouth full!' so much the better. Let the students demonstrate to the class how they can do several things at the same if at all possible.

3 Divide the class into pairs, distribute the worksheets and ask the students to discuss them.

4 The students report back for a whole class discussion of the most interesting parts of their conversations.

Are you someone who can easily do several things at the same time? Or are you a one thing at a time person? Discuss the following questions with your partner.

1 Can you make conversation while you:
   - cook?
   - feed the baby?
   - do odd jobs around the house?
   - programme the video recorder?

   Does it make a difference who you're talking to?

2 Can you listen to the radio and read?

3 Do you ever continue working on your computer or play computer games while talking on the phone?

4 Can you watch TV and read:
   - a book?
   - a magazine?
   - the newspaper?
   - a business letter or something else concerned with your job?
   - a personal letter?

5 Do you find it difficult to listen to what someone else is saying without forgetting what you want to say?

6 Can you pay attention at a meeting or lecture and at the same time do a crossword or knit?

7 Do you find it easy to work on several projects at the same time or do you prefer to work on one project at a time?

8 Do you read several books 'in parallel' or do you first finish one before starting the next?

9 Can you talk to more than one person about more than one subject at the same time?

10 Can you do a simple sum in your head while you read aloud? Try it and see!

Creating Conversation in Class © Chris Sion published by DELTA PUBLISHING

Making Connections

Level
Intermediate

Time
30 minutes

Language Function
Exchanging information

Materials
A good selection of 'connectors' such as glue, sticky tape, buttons, velcro, pins, string, paperclips, screws, drawing pins, zips, shoelaces and so on. If you have a large class, an overhead projector is useful

In Class

1 Bring in a selection of 'connectors' (see Materials) and teach the students the names of any items they don't know. If the class is too big for the students to see the objects clearly, put them on an overhead projector and you will get a beautifully magnified image of the objects themselves.

2 Ask the students what the objects have in common. Lead them towards the realisation that they are all systems of connecting. Ask them which other ways of joining, fastening or binding they can think of.

3 Now ask them to work in pairs and discuss which ways we have of making contact (i.e. connecting) with each other. Give them about five minutes and then let them report back to the whole class. Collect their ideas on the board. Prompt them if they can't think of anything. The sort of examples to expect might include some of the following:

sending a fax	smiling
writing a letter	phoning
sending an e-mail message	talking
inviting someone out	waving
dressing in a particular way	calling
giving a gift	shaking hands
asking the time	holding hands
asking for directions	kissing
offering a drink, sweet or cigarette	eye contact

4 What about the connections in the class? Tell the students their task is now to strengthen their connections with one of their classmates by talking to them. They should find a partner they'd like to get to know better and talk to them about whatever they like. If they can't think of anything to talk about, tell them to discuss some of the items on the board. The aim is to get to know each other better. Set a time limit of about ten or fifteen minutes.

5 Suggest to your students that they now select another student to talk to in English, this time as a homework activity. Leave the topic of conversation open but tell the students to try and make contact with classmates they don't speak to very often. Tell them that you will be asking them to report back next lesson. The aims here are making conversation in English and strengthening classroom contacts.

6 Students report back to the class at the next lesson or whenever contact has been made.

Personality Profile

Level
Intermediate

Time
45 minutes + several optional follow-up sessions of 30 minutes each (see NOTE 1)

Language Functions
Asking and answering questions; describing and reporting; exchanging personal information

Materials
Copies of both worksheets

In Class

1 Tell the students you are going to give them a personality questionnaire. What sort of people are they? To warm them up, ask for a show of hands. For example, who is:

generous   critical
friendly   selfish
sociable   sporting
shy   flexible
extrovert   fair
honest   cooperative

2 Continue by asking what other adjectives the class can think of to describe their personalities. Write the words up on the board and ask the students to spend a few minutes informally discussing which words they feel apply to themselves.

3 Divide the class into pairs and give out Worksheet 1. Tell the students to read through the questions and discuss a selection of the most interesting points with their partners. Set a time limit of about twenty minutes.

4 After the pairs have discussed the worksheet, ask for comments on some of the following issues:

● Which of the adjectives from Steps 1 and 2 would you now apply to yourself and your partner?

● Do you enjoy doing personality tests?

● Were there any items in the questionnaire that either irritated or amused you?

● Can you learn anything about yourself from a personality test?

● Which items on the profile do you feel give the best insight into a person's personality?

● Are there certain distinct personality types?

NOTE:

1 You may wish to spread the material over several lessons. Worksheet 2 is follow-up material which may be prepared at home for a later lesson or discussed directly in class.

2 Be warned that when it comes to the question of personality types, some students may fall back on negative racial and sexual stereotypes.

Read the questions and then discuss them with your partner.

1   Are you a well-organised person? Can you usually find your books, papers, clothes and so on easily?

2   In what situations are you prepared to lend people money? Do you ever borrow money from other people?

3   Do you mind lending your:
    - sports equipment?
    - CDs?
    - camera?
    - computer games?
    - videos?
    - books?
    - cooking utensils?
    - tools?
    - clothes?
    - bicycle?

4   Which of the items in Question 3 do you sometimes ask other people to lend you?

5   Do you point out other people's spelling mistakes or grammatical mistakes in your own language?

6   You've got a nasty bout of 'flu or even a bad cold. Do you:
    - go to work / school?
    - stay in bed?
    - stay at home but not in bed?
    - put on a brave face and carry on as usual?
    - carry on as usual but let everyone know you're not well?

7   At the counter of a bar or café, do you try and order first even though several other people were there before you?

8   If you are undercharged in a shop or restaurant, do you point it out or keep quiet?

9   Do you give money to registered charities and / or to beggars in the street?

10   You are in a queue waiting to pay at the supermarket. Your trolley is full. The customer just behind you has only one item. Do you offer to let them go first?

Creating Conversation in Class © Chris Sion published by DELTA PUBLISHING

Read the questions and then discuss them with your partner.

1 When you play a game, is it more important to you to win or to play well? Do you prefer an easy victory to a defeat that really challenges you but brings out the best in your game?

2 Can you keep a secret?

3 Do you ever drop in on people uninvited? Do you mind if other people drop in on you?

4 If a child asks you a riddle and you know the answer, do you pretend you don't know it so as not to spoil their fun?

5 Do you enjoy playing practical jokes? And can you take it and be a good sport when a practical joke is played on you?

6 What do you think of footballers who pretend they have been fouled and 'dive' in order to get a free kick?

7 Would you 'fix' the result of an important sports match if you can or do you believe in playing fair at all times?

8 Have you got a set routine for getting up in the morning? If so, describe it. How flexible are you if your routine is disturbed?

9 Would you report someone if you saw them copying in an exam?

10 Would you report someone if you saw them shoplifting?

Creating Conversation in Class © Chris Sion published by DELTA PUBLISHING

DOING IT IN ENGLISH

Sleep On It

Level: Elementary
Time: 20 minutes + a later session of 20 minutes
Language Function: Revising vocabulary
Materials: None

Before Class

Pick out some useful words and expressions you want the students to revise

In Class

1 Tell the students the words and expressions you want them to revise. Write them on the board and ask them if there is any other vocabulary they feel needs attention. Write their examples on the board, too, and explain anything that isn't clear.

2 Tell them to work individually and make a list of eight to ten words and expressions from those on the board that they want to work on.

3 Divide the class into pairs and tell them to exchange lists and spend a couple of minutes quizzing each other.

4 Explain the adage that 'The problem with learning a language is not remembering it but forgetting it'. Point out that one of the ways to counter the process of forgetting is to constantly work on what has been learned. Tell the students to spend the last five minutes of class selecting what vocabulary to work on. After class, they should go on to try some of the following techniques. Tell them that you will be asking them to report back on how they got on.

- Repeat the vocabulary to yourself once you are out of class. For example: while having lunch, waiting for the bus or walking to your car.

- Look over it once again when you get home.

- Tell somebody else, like a friend, family member or flat-mate, what the vocabulary is and explain it to them.

- Ask somebody to test you on it.

- Contact a friend, either by phone, fax, post or e-mail and tell them what you are trying to learn.

- Write the words on a piece of paper which you put just next to your bed or under your pillow. Be sure to look at it just as you are going to bed and then again first thing in the morning.

5 At the next lesson, ask the class to report back on what progress they have made.

NOTE: Although the main conversational element takes place only in Step 5, the activity provides a bridge between the classroom and the 'outside world' and you'll find that the students who do the tasks will have a great deal to say about them.

DOING IT IN ENGLISH

Thinking in English

Level: Intermediate
Time: 30 minutes + a later session of 10-15 minutes
Language Function: Reporting
Materials: None

Before Class
Select the material you want to revise

In Class

1 Spend a few minutes revising something you have recently covered in class.

2 Tell the students to repeat, quietly to themselves, what you have just revised in Step 1. They may do this repetition quietly, talking under their breath, or completely silently, 'in their heads'.

3 Now ask them to discuss in pairs to what extent they were able to think in English. Point out that being able to let go of thinking in their mother tongue in order to direct their thought processes into English represents a major step forwards.

4 Set the students the following simple homework activity. They should try repeating a couple of parts of the lesson to themselves quietly after class. The aim is to encourage them to try turning their thought processes into English. They should experiment and should try out different times and places to practise. For example: when going for a walk; doing the washing up; waiting for a bus; watering the garden; jogging; having a bath; or in bed before going to sleep.

5 At the next lesson ask the students to report back on their progress in thinking in English.

NOTE: Back up material may be found in: *Talking to Yourself in English* by Chris Sion (Training Etcetera) (Book 1 - Intermediate ISBN 90-74645-01-1; Book 2 - Advanced ISBN 90-74645-02-X)

5

Focusing on the Family

Whether they love them or hate them, most people will have something to say about their families: about their parents and children, uncles and aunts, cousins and grandparents. What are the most important family values in your family? What counts as good and bad behaviour? Who always seems to get their own way? Who gets blamed for everything? Who does the housework? No matter what sort of family you have, there is always a story to tell.

Fussy Parents

Level
    Intermediate

Time
    45 minutes

Language Functions
    Asking and answering questions;
    reflecting and reporting

Materials
    None

In Class

1 Tell your students you want to talk about getting up in the morning. As a warm up, ask them to list what parents have to do to get their children up and ready for school. For older students, can they remember what their parents used to do? They can work individually, in pairs or small groups. Their lists should be as detailed as possible but may include general or specific activities. For example:

clean teeth	wash face
put lid on toothpaste	dry hands
get dressed	eat breakfast
put on T-shirt	drink milk

2 Write their examples on the board and tell them to select ten to fifteen of them and write them down.

3 Divide the class into pairs, A and B: A is the fussy parent, B the child. You might like to ask for a volunteer to demonstrate for the class first.

4 The situation is as follows: The child is asleep. The parent wakes him / her up and starts asking a range of questions based on the examples selected in Step 2:

- What do you want to wear today?
- Do you think that's warm enough?
- Have you cleaned your teeth?
- Where are your shoes?
- What do you want for breakfast?
- Are you sure that's enough?
- Have you done your homework?
- Where did you put your books?

The parent should ask each of the questions several times, referring to their notes at first if necessary, but later without looking at them. The child should answer at times politely, at times distractedly, at times impatiently.

5 The pairs should now discuss their reactions to playing the role of parent or child. How did they feel in the roles? Were the parents authoritarian, patient, loving or overly fussy? Were the children well-behaved and polite, or rebellious and aggressive?

6 The students now exchange roles.

7 Finish off by discussing getting up in the morning. Who does what, when and for whom, in your family? Has anyone got a strict morning routine? What is the best way to upset you in the morning? What can you do to get yourself (and everyone else) off to a good start each day?

Bad Behaviour

Level

Intermediate

Time

30-45 minutes

Language Functions

Describing and narrating; evaluating; expressing moral preferences

Materials

Copies of the worksheet

In Class

1 Explain that the word 'naughty' means badly behaved and disobedient, and say that you are going to talk about naughty children. Ask what sort of behaviour students associate with being naughty. For example: being cheeky or disrespectful; being immoral; being a threat to yourself, to others or to property.

2 Tell the students to try to think of specific examples of being naughty, and write them on the board.

3 Divide the class into pairs and tell them to discuss the following points. Encourage them to think of specific examples of what they mean.

- Which of the examples on the board do you think are the worst / least bad behaviour?

- What was the naughtiest thing you ever did as a child? Was it really so bad? Who told you it was naughty? Do you regret it? Would you find it acceptable if a child of yours did it today?

- What is the difference between being naughty, being badly behaved and being just a bit mischievous? Does it depend on how old you are, where you are or who you are with?

4 The students then briefly report back to the whole class.

5 Hand out copies of the worksheet and explain that you are going to consider the question of reward and punishment. Students discuss the questions in pairs and then compare answers around the class.

Read the following questions and discuss and your answers in pairs.

- Which punishments are suitable for which behaviour?
  (Use the examples on the board or any others you can think of.)

- What is the value of punishment?

- What should you do if a punishment proves to be totally ineffective?

- How are / were you punished at school?

- How are / were you punished at home?

- How are / were you rewarded for good behaviour at school?

- What sorts of rewards are / were you given at home?

- Do you think children should be praised and rewarded for good behaviour?
  Or is it simply to be expected of them?

- Which rewards motivate you best?

- All in all, do you feel you are / were fairly treated?

Creating Conversation in Class © Chris Sion published by DELTA PUBLISHING

Can We Go Swimming?

Level
Intermediate

Time
30-45 minutes

Language Functions
Making requests; refusing and giving in to requests

Materials
None

In Class

1 Divide the class into two groups. One group is to play the part of the parents. The other group are the children. Brief them as follows:

Children: Make a list of things you would like to have or do, such as going swimming, playing monopoly, buying a new computer game, playing hide and seek and so on.

Parents: Think of as many ways as you can of responding to children's requests, both positively and negatively. For example:

- Of course you can!
- Alright.
- No, not now.
- Another time.
- Later.
- Okay, just this once.
- Can't you see I'm busy?
- Perhaps.
- Ask your father.
- First finish your homework.
- I'm not in the mood today.
- What a good idea!

2 Ask the groups to report back and write a selection of their examples on the board.

3 Each parent should now pair off with a child. The children should ask the parents for some of the things they listed in Step 1. The adults' task is initially to refuse the request and then, finally, to give in. As soon as a request is complied with, the child should make the next request. For example:

Child: Can we go to the circus today?
Parent: What did you say?
Child: *Please* can we go to the circus today?
Parent: No, not today.
Child: Can we go tomorrow? Pretty please?
Parent: Perhaps. But first tidy your room.
Child: I have tidied my room. Please, please, *please*?
Parent: Yes, alright. Let's go.
Child: Thank you! Can I have some popcorn at the circus?
Parent: Do you know how much it costs? It's expensive ...

4 The adults and children reverse roles.

5 Finish off with a general discussion of children and the older generation in the modern world. Some points you might want to discuss are:

- Are children better or worse off today than a generation ago?

- What does it mean to 'spoil' a child?

- How can parents cope with 'pester power' (the power children have to nag their parents to buy them things)?

You Can't Win

Level
Intermediate

Time
45-60 minutes

Language Functions
Requesting and giving help, advice, permission and opinions; disagreeing and contradicting; reporting

Materials
None

In Class

1 Divide the class into groups of four, in which one student plays the part of the father, one the student plays the mother and two students are the children in a family.

2 Tell the parents to work together and build up personality profiles of themselves. They should base the profiles on as many contradictory values as they can. For example: if Dad is religious, Mum is an atheist; Mum is a meat eater, Dad is a vegetarian; Mum is frugal, Dad is extravagant; Mum likes Agassi, Dad likes Sampras; Mum is happy with white lies (and not such white lies), Dad believes honesty is the best policy.

3 While the parents are working, tell the children to decide on their age and then make a list of appropriate requests to ask their parents. These points may be requesting permission to do something, asking for guidance, asking an opinion and so on. For example:

- Can I go camping in the South of France?

- Can I stay up late tonight?

- Should I become a vegetarian?

- Do you like my new hairstyle?

4 Tell the children to make their various requests of their parents. The parents should consistently contradict each other in replying.

5 Get students to report a selection of their parents' reactions to the whole class. Encourage them to talk about how they felt when confronted with the contradictions.

6 Finally, divide the class into pairs and ask them to discuss the following points:

- Did your parents ever contradict themselves in bringing you up?

- Do they do so today?

- If you are a parent, do you and your partner ever treat your children this way? Would your partner agree with your answer?

- Do you think it is important for parents to agree about everything to do with their children (discipline, presents, permission and so on)?

Jack Sprat

Level
Intermediate

Time
30-45 minutes

Language Functions
Describing; comparing; giving personal information; expressing opinions; asking and answering questions; contradicting

Materials
None

In Class

1 Ask if anyone knows the nursery rhyme 'Jack Sprat' and write it up on the board:

Jack Sprat would eat no fat
His wife would eat no lean
And so betwixt them both
They licked the platter clean

Ask if they can guess the meaning. Explain that although Jack and his wife are completely different they complement each other.

2 Divide the class into pairs, ideally of a male and a female student. Tell them to write a short description of Jack Sprat and his wife. Ask them to make them as different as possible and emphasise the contrast. For example:

Jack Sprat: *47 – likes chamber music – collects stamps – not very tall – well built – comes from a large family – parents divorced – pacifist ...*

Jacqui Sprat: *74 – likes rock 'n roll - carpentry – 6 ft tall – chubby (she eats all the fat) – only child – close family – served in the navy during the war ...*

3 The students read out their descriptions and discuss whose characters were the best.

4 Tell two pairs of students to work together, Pair A and Pair B. Each pair should prepare some questions to ask the other pair. They should then take turns at role playing the Sprats as follows: In Pair A, one student is Jack and the other Jacqui Sprat. Pair B should ask them questions, which they answer contradictorily, just as the Sprats would. For example:

Pair B student: Do you think it's going to rain?
Jack: Doesn't look like rain.
Jacqui: Well, the forecast said it would rain.

Pair B student: When should I buy my new computer?
Jacqui: I'd buy it today if I were you.
Jack: You must be mad! You should wait till the price comes down.

Pay attention to stress patterns. The contradictions cannot be adequately expressed in a monotone!

5 The pairs exchange roles, so that Pair B plays the part of the Sprats and Pair A asks the questions.

6 Tell the students to stay in their groups to discuss the following points:

- Do you know any couples who are 'chalk and cheese'? You need not restrict yourself to married couples. You could also talk about a brother and sister, two classmates or two colleagues who work together. Describe them.

- Do you think that radically different personalities are a source of unavoidable conflict or do they complement each other?

Family Values

Level
Intermediate

Time
30-60 minutes

Language Functions
Expressing moral preferences;
recalling the past; expressing conditions

Materials
None

In Class

1 Ask the students what they would do when confronted with some simple everyday moral choices. For example, what if:

- they saw a group of teenagers vandalising a tree?

- they noticed a fellow student copying during an exam?

- an acquaintance asked them to borrow some money?

- they saw a child being bullied in the school playground?

- they found £100 in the street?

2 Ask them if they can think of other examples and note them in a couple of words on the board ('vandalising tree', 'copying in exam' and so on).

3 Divide the class into pairs and tell the students to discuss what they or members of their families would do in the situations on the board. They may also refer to actual situations they have experienced. What did they do, and why?

4 Tell the students to think about the most important values in their families. What are / were those values? Write them up on the board. For example:

- Be kind to animals.
- Don't despise people less fortunate than yourself.
- Waste not, want not.
- Respect your elders.
- Boys don't cry.
- Always say please and thank you.
- A promise is a promise.
- Neither a borrower nor a lender be.
- Play fair.
- Don't be ungrateful.
- Stick up for yourself.
- Love your neighbour.
- Forgive your enemies.

5 Tell the students to discuss the following points with their partners, as appropriate:

- Which of the above values are taught in your family? (For teenage students)

- Which of the above values were you taught as a child? (For adults)

- Which of the values do you agree / disagree with?

- Which would you (or do you) teach your children?

6 Finish off by asking the students one by one to say which three values they personally believe to be the most important.

NOTE: The values I have listed in Step 4 are generally positive, but bear in mind that you might be confronted with other controversial examples with an ethnic, sexist or religious dimension.

It's All Your Fault

<table>
<tr><td>

Level
Intermediate

Time
30 minutes

Language Functions
Blaming and accusing; making conditional
statements; reporting

Materials
None

</td></tr>
</table>

In Class

1 Discuss briefly with the class how we often
blame each other quite unfairly for a whole range
of reasons. Then brainstorm language associated
with blaming. For example:

- It's your fault! Don't blame me!
- Now look what you've done!
- Of course, I'm not *blaming* you!
- If it hadn't been for you it would never have
  happened!
- Can't you ever do anything right?

Point out the importance of intonation and body
language. It's not only what you say, it's *how* you
say it.

2 Tell the students to work in pairs and then report
back to the class. Their task is to think of as many
unpleasant and negative incidents as they can.
Collect the examples on the board in note form.
The range should extend from simple everyday
incidents to 'cosmic' disasters. For example:

- lost my bus ticket
- plague sweeps through Europe
- car wouldn't start
- gained five kilos

- knocking over bottle of wine
- washing machine broken
- Concorde disaster

Remember that in a class of mixed nationalities
there might be considerable disagreement about
the causes of historical events. Restrict yourself to
trivial examples if there is a risk of tension.

3 Now tell the students you are going to give them
the chance to practise blaming each other for
having been responsible for the incidents on the
board. They may also add whichever other ones
they please. Tell them to try to remember what
they were blamed for so they can report back to
the class later. They should build up a
conversation, which should be amusing and
completely irrational but avoiding genuine
confrontation. It might go something like this:

A: It's your fault I lost my wallet!
B: How can you say it was my fault? I told you
not to keep it in your back pocket. Anyway, if
it hadn't been for you I wouldn't have got a
parking ticket.
A: Don't blame me for that.
B: You wanted to take the car ...

4 Tell the students to report back on what they
were blamed for. How did they feel about the
accusations?

5 Divide the class into pairs and tell them to
discuss the following points:

- Do you know anyone who frequently blames
  other people unreasonably?
- Do you blame others unfairly yourself?
- Have you ever been blamed for something you
  didn't do?
- Is there a scapegoat where you work or at your
  school?

Housework

Level
Intermediate

Time
20-30 minutes

Language Functions
Expressing preferences; expressing frequency

Materials
None

In Class

1 Start a list on the board of all the household chores you can think of and elicit further examples from the students. Make the list as detailed as possible and include both general and specific examples. For example:

- cooking
- loading and emptying the dishwasher
- emptying the wastepaper bins
- washing up the pots and pans
- making the beds
- changing the bedclothes
- dusting
- hoovering
- washing
- folding up clean washing
- ironing
- sewing on buttons
- doing odd-jobs around the house
- locking up at night
- cleaning the windows
- spring cleaning
- making tea or coffee
- setting the table
- clearing away after meals
- tidying up
- cleaning the bathroom and toilet
- making sandwiches for school

2 Divide the class into pairs and tell them to discuss some or all of the following points:

- Who does which household chores in your family?
- Which chores do the members of your family most / least like?
- Which chores do you do?
- Which do you most and least like?
- Do you ever ask for help?
- Are you ever asked to help?
- What could make the chores more tolerable, for example: listening to the radio or doing chores together?

3 Finish off with a class vote. Which chores are the most popular? Which are the least?

DOING TESTS AND EXAMINATIONS

Examining Exams

Level: Intermediate

Time: 30-45 minutes

Language Functions: Reporting; evaluating; expressing opinions

Materials: Copies of the worksheet

In Class

1 Tell the class to close their books and take a pen and some paper, as they are going to have an exam. Clean the board, look serious and add a few further details, such as that the principal of the school has introduced a new policy stating that students who fail the exam will have to pay a fine if they want to continue the course. Expect long faces, complaints and a good measure of resistance.

2 You can now tell the students you were only joking! What a relief! Spend a few minutes discussing the students' reactions with them. What exactly were they afraid of? What sort of questions did they feel they could, and could not, have answered? What did they feel confident about? What do they feel about tests and exams in general?

3 Tell them that you are going to talk about the value of examinations. Now that they have discussed their feelings about them, what words do they associate with exams?

Write the words up on the board. Elicit as much vocabulary as possible. For example:

nerves	crib
test	swot
mark	pressure
examiner	time
invigilator	oral exam
candidate	written exam
learn parrot fashion	(not) fair
learn by heart	fear of failure
insomnia	practical
nightmare	re-sit
copy	fail
cheat	pass

Remind the students that you can 'sit', 'write', 'take' or even 'do' an exam. However, to 'make' an exam is not correct English. Moreover, they get 'marks', not 'notes'.

4 Divide the class into pairs and ask them to spend five minutes discussing the advantages and disadvantages of examinations.

5 Give out the worksheet and tell the students to discuss a selection of items on it and then report back on what they found the most interesting points. You might like to cover both parts of the worksheet separately and at different times. There is a lot to talk about!

Discuss some of the following points with your partner:

Your personal experience

- Do you get nervous before exams?

- Your last exam: what result did you expect and what did you get?

- How do you prepare for exams?

- Do you always read the questions carefully in a written exam?

- Have you ever been unfairly treated in an exam?

- Have you ever cheated in an exam?

- If you saw another student cheating in an exam, would you report them?

- Would you help another student who asked for assistance during an exam?

Your opinions

- Are exams a necessary evil?

- Do exams motivate students to give their best?

- What do you think of alternatives to exams, such as projects and continuous assessment?

- Would you agree that exams are only really valuable if you are allowed to see your paper once it has been marked, so you can learn from your mistakes?

- Should you be given warning before an exam? Why (not)?

- Should dictionaries and other reference books be permitted during exams? Why (not)?

- Should you be allowed to repeat an exam if you fail? If so, how often?

- Should attendance at a course always be required in order to take an exam?

Creating Conversation in Class © Chris Sion published by DELTA PUBLISHING

6

Playing Games

Games represent a pleasant, informal means of getting your students interacting in English. Although enjoyable, their value in teaching English is not to be taken lightly. When students are playing a game, their focus of attention shifts away from language skills, which enables them to learn effectively at the same time as having fun.

Games are a serious business! Although they usually start with a basic framework of rules, they frequently go on to create a great deal of unstructured conversation in a lively English language classroom.

Even those which are not specifically language games can generate a lot to talk about. They are not just amusing, they involve authentic conversation. Several of the ones included here were developed by me and my family at home. I can recommend them.

If You Were an Elephant

<table>
<tr><td>

Level

Intermediate

Time

20 minutes + 15 minutes in a later lesson
for Step 5

Language Functions

Expressing consequences; comparing
and describing

Materials

None

</td></tr>
</table>

In Class

1 Tell the class to think of as many different
animals as they can and write them up on the
board.

2 Divide the class into pairs, A and B, and explain
the game, as follows: A states the name of an
animal. B makes a conditional sentence about A
and the animal, along the lines of, 'If you were
a ... , I'd ...' It is then B's turn to state the name of
an animal while A has to make the conditional
sentence. For example:

A: Elephant
B: If you were an elephant, I'd ride on your
back.

B: Snake
A: If you were a snake, I'd make a belt from your
skin.

A: Dog
B: If you were a dog, I'd give you a bone and
take you for a walk.

3 Ask each student to tell the class the best
example of what their partner said:

'Rosemary said that if I were a frog, she'd kiss me
to see if I would turn into a prince.'

'Claudia said that if I were an octopus, she'd fill
her pen with my ink.'

4 Now tell the students to each assume the identity
of an animal. Their task is to engage in
unstructured conversation with each other. They
can discuss anything they like. A good starting
point is for them to describe and compare
themselves in their animal identities. If at all
possible you should let them move round the
classroom, using their bodies as much as their
voices to express themselves.

5 To follow up the game at a later lesson, you can
try famous people or objects instead of animals.
For example:

A: John Lennon
B: If you were John Lennon, I'd ask you to sing
me a song.

A: Book
B: If you were a book, I'd read you.

Guessing Game

Level

Intermediate

Time

30-60 minutes depending on the Additional Options selected

Language Functions

Asking and answering questions; classifying and comparing

Materials

Small pieces of paper; for Additional Option C, you need a large classroom in which the students can move around easily

Before Class

Write the names of some games on small pieces of paper to use as prompts in Step 2

In Class

1 Explain that the aim is for one student to think of a game and for the others to ask closed questions to establish what it is. Any game at all may be selected, from chess or noughts & crosses to basketball, bridge or badminton. Begin by doing an example with the whole class. The sort of questions to expect are:

- Is it a board game?
- Is it a ball game?
- Is it a team game?
- Do you play it indoors?
- Is it expensive to play?
- Do you need any equipment?
- Can **you** play this game?
- Have you played it recently?
- Do they broadcast it on TV?
- Is it popular in this country?

The students need not take turns to ask their questions but make sure that everyone is involved. Give them a couple of clues if they get stuck. For example:

- There are eleven players in a team.
- You usually play for money.
- It is one of the Olympic games.
- The world championships took place last year.

2 Divide the class into small groups and tell them to start the activity and enjoy themselves. If students run out of ideas, whisper an example in their ear or give them a slip of paper with the name of the game written on it.

Additional Options

A Write a list of all the games that have been used so far, as examples, up on the board. Tell the class to work individually and classify the games into categories such as: board games; ball games; racket games; outdoor games; team games; and so on. Then tell the students to discuss their classifications with a partner.

B Tell the students to work in pairs and discuss: the games they play; when, where and with whom they play games; games played by friends and family; the games they are best and worst at and so on.

C Call out the name of a game, for example, 'SQUASH!' Students who play squash should gather on one side of the class while students who don't play gather on the other. Continue by introducing 'often', 'sometimes', 'never', 'hardly ever' or 'occasionally'. The students should now group themselves according to how frequently they play squash. This always generates a lot of discussion.

Say 'Yes'

Level
Advanced

Time
30 minutes

Language Functions
Asking and answering questions; practising emphatic forms; expressing consequences

Materials
None

In Class

1 Divide the class into pairs, A and B. Their task is to write ten to twenty questions each to ask their partner. They should write closed questions (i.e. ones that can be answered 'Yes' or 'No'). Encourage them to think up a good mix of questions referring to facts, opinions and feelings. They should also try to use a variety of different question openers such as 'Can', 'Should', 'Do', 'Was' and so on. The easiest way of generating a lot of interesting questions is to provide a large number of examples yourself:

- Can you fly through the air?

- Should I take my umbrella?

- Does water boil at 95º?

- Was Picasso a great artist?

- Do you like ice-cream?

- Do dogs moo?

- Is milk blue?

- Can I come to your birthday party?

- Would you like a drink?

- Does smoking damage your health?

2 Give the students about fifteen minutes to write their questions. Check that the language is correct and help students who cannot easily find suitable ideas.

3 In each pair, A quickly checks that he / she understands B's questions. A should not answer the questions at this stage but should just check that they are clear.

4 B repeats the questions and this time A must answer 'Yes!' to all the questions. Where 'Yes' is not the answer one would normally expect, A should answer like someone who always wants to have the last word. Where necessary, A should explain or qualify their answer. For example:

- Yes, I can fly if I get in a plane.

- Yes, water does boil at 95º if the air pressure's low enough.

- Yes, dogs do moo if they imitate cows.

- Yes, milk is blue if you see it in blue light or if you mix it with ink.

5 A and B reverse roles with A asking B his / her questions.

Picture Gallery

Level

Intermediate

Time

30 minutes

Language Function

Making connections

Materials

Old magazines and newspapers; scissors; glue; photocopies of line drawings

Before Class

Cut a selection of line drawings or illustrations that photocopy well out of some old newspapers or magazines. It's a good idea to build up a bank of these little drawings. Pick about eight to use with your class. Mount them on a piece of paper, number them and photocopy them. Include some pictures that are obviously connected with what you want to talk about and some with no apparent connection at all.

In Class

1 Give the students the copies you have prepared and discuss the content. Prompt them with lots of questions such as:

- Who is she?
- What are they doing?
- What's going to happen next?
- What's she holding in her left hand?
- What are they thinking?
- What do you think is happening just beyond the part of the picture we can see?

2 Tell the students to think of some ideas for relating the drawings to aspects of their lives such as work, school, hobbies, home, a problem they're trying to solve and so on. Give them about ten minutes for this step. Tell them to be as inventive as they like. Give a couple of examples yourself so they are clear about exactly what you mean.

3 When they are ready, tell the students to share their ideas either in pairs, small groups or as a whole class.

Heads or Tails?

Level
Intermediate

Time
15-20 minutes

Language Functions
Asking questions; predicting the future

Materials
One coin (with heads and tails) for each pair of students

In Class

1 Discuss the convention of spinning a coin with the class. When do we spin a coin? Did the students know we call 'Heads or tails?' Are there heads on the coins in their countries? What do they call 'spinning a coin' in their countries? Do any of the students ever spin a coin in making a decision?

2 Tell the students you want them to play a game based on spinning a coin. The game is to ask closed questions and spin the coin to see what answer it gives. The questions should be spontaneous rather than prepared and relate to the members of the class, but should avoid morbid subjects like death, disease or disaster.

3 Establish a convention, for example: that heads is 'Yes' and tails is 'No', and give a demonstration from the front of the class. Suitable questions are:

- Should we have a break now?
- Should the class go to the cinema together on Saturday?
- Will Roland be here on Friday afternoon?
- Will Felix win his next tennis match?
- Will Katya become a great ballet dancer?
- Should we watch a video after lunch?
- Should smoking be banned in the cafeteria?

4 Let the students ask you some questions and see what the coin answers. If you don't like the response you can always ask the coin, 'Are you sure?', 'Are you absolutely positive?' until you get the answer you want!

5 Divide the class into pairs and give each pair a coin. Tell them to have fun and take turns at spinning the coin and asking it questions.

6 Ask the students to report back on what questions they asked and what the coins answered.

Thingamajigs

Level

Elementary

Time

15 minutes

Language Functions

Describing; circumlocuting; clarifying and interpreting

Materials

A variety of small objects and a bag to put them in. The sorts of objects I have used are listed below:

rubber or metal washer	safety pin
toothpick	key ring
pair of tweezers	stapler
envelope	floppy disk
typewriter ribbon	pencil sharpener
stamp	mousetrap

In Class

1 Bring a selection of small objects into the class in a bag so that the students cannot see them. Ideally, you need enough objects for each student to be able to participate. In big classes, you can prepare a list and whisper the object to each student. Explain that the aim of the activity is to learn to ask for things when you don't know the name. Each student will get a turn to ask for a small object as if they were customers in a shop. The rest of the class are shopkeepers.

2 Give the 'customers' the language they need, depending on their level. For example:

- Can you help me, please?
- Do you think you could help me, please?
- I wonder whether you could help me, please?
- I'm afraid I don't know the English word for what I want.
- I'm looking for one of those (funny) little things for ... -ing ...
- I don't know what the English word is but I want something for ... -ing ...
- I want one of those little things that ...

3 Give the students the objects one by one. The rest of the class should not be able to see the objects. Tell the student whose turn it is that even if they know the name of their object, they should confine themselves to a description of it and its function. However, they should explain what they want the object for. The students playing the part of the shopkeepers should ask questions to try and establish what the objects are. Help them with the precise vocabulary where necessary. If the exchanges go too quickly, tell the shopkeepers to pretend they don't understand and make it a little more difficult for the customers.

NOTE: 'Thingamajig' is a word you use when you can't find the word you want.

This and That

<table>
<tr><td>

Level
   Intermediate

Time
   30-40 minutes

Language Functions
   Comparing and describing

Materials
   None

</td></tr>
</table>

In Class

1 Write a selection of about twenty concrete nouns on the board and elicit some further examples from the students. For example:

grandfather	jar
toothbrush	calculator
church	vase
hockey stick	computer
car	haircut
children	bell
garden	electricity
rose	watch
tennis racquet	postcard
flying saucer	badge

2 Check that the students know what the words mean.

3 Divide the class into pairs and tell them you want them to talk about, and compare, a selection of items on the list. For example:

A: My grandfather is 87. He lives in Brighton. He used to be a plumber.

B: My grandfather died a couple of years ago. I never knew him well. He lived in Paris.

A: My other grandfather is also dead but I knew him really well. He used to live around the corner from us. I used to see him almost every day …

Items which seem inappropriate, such as 'flying saucer', can still be included and, rather than simply ignoring them, you can stretch students' imaginations thinking of an amusing or creative means of comparing them. Explain that the idea behind the exercise is to use the comparisons as a starting point for talking about a wide range of everyday subjects. The students should try to develop a free conversation, not close it down with the shortest possible answers.

Morris and Boris

<table>
<tr><td>

Level
Elementary

Time
15-20 minutes + 15-20 minutes for Step 5 in a later lesson

Language Functions
Comparing and describing

Materials
None

</td></tr>
</table>

In Class

1 Draw two simple figures on the board making sure that their features are clearly different. The more features you include, the greater the scope for making comparisons. My characters are called Morris and Boris:

Morris

Boris

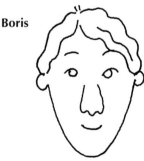

2 Tell the students to work in pairs and make as many comparative sentences about Morris and Boris as they can. For example:

- Morris's mouth is bigger than Boris's.
- Boris's nose is longer than Morris's.
- Morris looks less cheerful than Boris.
- Boris is thinner than Morris.
- Boris has a bigger smile than Morris.
- Morris is fatter than Boris.

3 Ask each student to give a couple of examples comparing the two figures.

4 Finish off by asking the students, either in pairs or as a group, to look around the class and make further comparisons. For example:

A: Jim's watch is more expensive than mine.
B: Is it really? It doesn't look very expensive.

A: Today's warmer than yesterday.
B: No, it isn't. I'm freezing.

A: Janet is older than Victoria.
B: Yes, and she's taller too.

A: Linda knows more jokes than you do.
B: No, she doesn't. I just don't like telling jokes.

5 Follow up at a subsequent lesson by asking each student to draw, for example, a house, a plant or a dog. Reassure students who are concerned about not being able to draw well that a rough sketch is all that's required. Their task is then to compare these drawings in pairs.

Odd Man Out

Level
Intermediate

Time
30 minutes

Language Function
Comparing

Materials
None

In Class

1 Read out the following sets of four items and ask the students to say which is the odd man out in each set. You can either proceed set by set, discussing the answers one by one, or read out all the sets, telling the students to note their answers and discussing it only at the end.

- snow, coal, milk, Tipp-Ex

- car, caravan, tent, bicycle

- feet, eyes, ears, teeth

- pen, chalk, ruler, pencil

- scorpion, cat, dog, goldfish

When you discuss the answers, ask first what would probably be expected if the items were found in a conventional intelligence test. For example, in the first set, 'coal' would be the exception because the others are all white. Then go on to ask whether there are other ways of interpreting the answer. For example, 'snow' could be the exception because the other three are commodities which you can buy. Or 'milk' could be the answer because milk is the only one of the four you drink. Any suggestions for Tipp-Ex?

2 Tell the students to work in pairs. Their task is to think of a couple of similar examples of sets of four words each containing an exception. Point out that the more imaginative their examples and the more open to different interpretations they are, the more they will be able to say about them.

3 Going round the class, get the pairs one by one to ask the other students to indicate the odd men out from their sets. Encourage discussion of the answers.

NOTE: I should like to acknowledge that I got the basic idea behind 'Odd Man Out' from Jacqueline Stoker's 'Word Quiz Book' (Paperfront).

News Quiz

Level

Intermediate

Time

30-45 minutes + a later session of 45 minutes

Language Functions

Reporting; asking questions

Materials

None

Before Class

Prepare a news quiz based on current events. Choose questions in line with the interests and level of your students. Include a good mixture of questions referring to politics (local, national and international), culture, business, sport and so on.

In Class

1 Ask the students the questions you have prepared.

2 Tell them to work in pairs and allow about ten minutes for discussing the following questions:

- Do you try to keep up to date with what's happening in the world?

- What is your main source of news information - newspaper, radio, or TV?

- Is there any particular topic you have been following on the news recently?

- What do you feel about the news and how it's presented in general?

3 Brainstorm categories of news. For example: local news; current affairs; sports; business; culture and so on.

4 Tell the students each to select one category from Step 3 and to prepare three quiz questions based on recent news before the next lesson. Make sure the categories are equally shared out so you get approximately the same number of questions in each category. Tell the students that they should make a point of following the news at least until the next lesson so they will be able to answer questions and prepare their own. Stress that the questions should not be too difficult. They should use English language media if they can. If they can't, they will have to translate from sources in other languages.

5 In the next lesson, tell the students to form groups according to the category they chose in Step 4. They should prepare a combined group list of about ten questions on their category. They should try to include at least one question from each member of the group. Circulate, helping with language problems and, if necessary, filtering out questions which are too obscure.

6 The groups ask their questions and the others answer them if they can. You may wish to introduce a points system if you have a competitive class but this is by no means essential.

7 Finish off by asking the students to work in pairs and discuss some of the news items that have come up in the quiz.

Take Ten

Level
Elementary

Time
20-30 minutes

Language Function
Practising vocabulary

Materials
None

In Class

1 Tell the class you are going to give them a subject and they should try and write down about ten examples of it. They can work alone or in pairs. Suitable subjects could be:

things you can put on a pizza
things you can put on a sandwich
things you can eat
drinks
colours
languages
trees
cities
Olympic sports
countries
short forms of names
school rules
things that use batteries
things you see on an aeroplane
parts of the body
things you see in a circus
parts of the body you can't see
flowers
computer terms
multinational companies
professions
jobs for which you have to wear a uniform

things you find in a hospital
opposites
musical instruments
things that can melt
plays by Shakespeare
operas
pop groups with English names
composers

2 Give the students the subject and tell them how long they have to complete the task. Both the subjects you choose and the time will vary with the level and interests of the class.

3 Ask round the class for at least one example from each student. Make sure that everybody gets a chance to contribute. Keep the pace brisk.

4 Repeat a couple of times with different subjects.

5 Divide the class into teams of three or four students. Select five subjects such as those listed in Step 1. Be sure to pick subjects that are relevant to the students' interests and are at the correct level. Set a time limit and tell them their task is to think of ten examples of each subject.

6 When the time has elapsed, go round the class listening to the students' lists. Encourage them to argue about unusual examples and borderline cases. Would you really want a banana sandwich? If the students want a scoring system, discuss which form it should take. The simplest is to give each correct contribution a point. Make sure that all students are involved both in thinking up examples and in reporting on them to the class.

NOTE: This activity is based on the game *Outburst*.

professional perspectives

professional perspectives is a series of practical methodology
books designed to provide teachers of English with fresh insights,
innovative ideas and original classroom materials.

Other titles in the series include:

Talking Business in Class
by Chris Sion
More than 50 engaging activities to provide free-stage
conversation in professional classes

Humanising your Coursebook
by Mario Rinvolucri
A wide range of activities designed to extend typical
coursebook language practice by engaging students
creatively and productively

The MINIMAX Teacher
by Jon Taylor
Practical, easy-to-use activities that generate the
maximum student output from the minimum teacher
input

Using the Mother Tongue
by Sheelagh Deller and Mario Rinvolucri
Ready-to-use activities which make creative use of
the students' mother tongue in the language learning
classroom

Unlocking Self-expression through NLP
by Judith Baker and Mario Rinvolucri
Over 100 speaking activities which draw on the
insights into communication provided by
Neuro-Linguistic Programming

Spontaneous Speaking
by David Heathfield
A series of drama activities which promote positive
classroom dynamics, build confidence and lead to
improved fluency

The *Resourceful* English Teacher
by Jonathan Chandler and Mark Stone
A complete teaching companion containing 200
classroom activities for use in a wide range of
teaching situations

For a full list and further details of titles
in the *professional perspectives* series,
contact the publishers at:

DELTA PUBLISHING
39 Alexandra Road
Addlestone
Surrey KT15 2PQ

Tel +44 (0)1932 854776
Fax +44 (0)1932 849528
E-mail info@deltapublishing.co.uk
Web www.deltapublishing.co.uk